The Search For Significance

Information for the corresponding Small Group Leader's Guide is at the back of this book

Robert S. McGee

REVISION

**Copyright © 1987
Robert S. McGee**

BOOK ISBN:0-945276-00-1
BOOK & WORKBOOK ISBN:0-945276-01-X

Robert S. McGee
P.O. Box 580355, Houston, Texas 77258

To my wife, Marilyn, who has given of herself so that I might minister these truths, both personally and now by the written word.

ACKNOWLEDGMENTS

These concepts have been utilized at our counseling centers and seminars for many years. The results have been so phenomenal that we were compelled to produce this book. Many have contributed so that The Search For Significance could be produced. I want to especially single out my staff, whose great dedication to the spreading of these truths is immeasurable. I also want to thank Rick Hove, Ray Anderson, Melanie Ahlquists, Dan Hayes, Conrad Koch, Richard Price, Jay Hamman, Becky Blount, and especially my mother, Minerva McGee, all of whom have made significant contributions to this book. Finally, I would like to thank Pat Springle who was instrumental in bringing clarity and insight into this material.

INTRODUCTION

When Christ told His disciples, *"You shall know the truth and the truth shall set you free" (John 8:32),* He wasn't referring only to an intellectual assent to the truth. He was referring to the application of truth in the most basic issues of life: our goals, our motives, and our sense of self-worth. Unfortunately, many of us give only lip-service to the powerful truths of the Scriptures without allowing them to radically affect the basis of our self-worth. Instead, we continue to seek our security and purpose from the world's sources: personal success, status, beauty, wealth, and the approval of others. These may fulfill for a short time, but soon they lead to a sense of urgency to succeed and be approved again.

To meet these compelling needs, we are driven to succeed, we do virtually anything to make people happy with us, and we spend countless hours and dollars trying to look "just right." Also, we avoid situations and people where the risk of failure and rejection is too high. It's a rat race that can't be won by simply running faster. We need to get off the hopeless treadmill and learn to apply the foundational truths that can set us free and motivate us to live for Christ.

Christ's death paid the penalty for our sins, and His resurrection gives us new life, new goals, and new hope. He has given us complete security and challenging purpose that are not based on our abilities. They are based on His grace and the power of His Spirit. Yes, Christ wants us to be intense and ambitious, but not about our success or status. If we understand His forgiveness and acceptance, we will be intense about the right things - Christ and His cause - and we will be free to enjoy His love.

This is the fifth edition of the material presented in The Search For Significance, and the response of those who have read the book and used the workbook has been overwhelming. I hope the Lord will use them to convince you of His love, forgiveness, and purposes for your life.

"For the love of Christ controls us, having concluded this, that one died for all, therefore all died; and He died for all, that they who live should no longer live for themselves, but for Him who died and rose again on their behalf" (II Corinthians 5:14-15).

Sincerely,
Robert S. McGee

TABLE OF CONTENTS

"I must meet certain standards to feel good about myself..."

Fear of Failure Test

The Effects of the Fear of Failure

God's Answer: Justification

A Beginning Exercise

"I must be approved by certain others to feel good about myself..."

Fear of Rejection Test

The Effects of the Fear of Rejection

God's Answer: Reconciliation

A Beginning Exercise

"Those who fail are unworthy of love and deserve to be punished."

Fear of Punishment Test

The Effects of the Fear of Punishment

God's Answer: Propitiation

A Beginning Exercise

"I am what I am; I cannot change; I am hopeless"

Shame Test

Chapter One

Our Search for Significance

Relatively few of us experience the blend of contentment and godly intensity that God intends for each person. From life's outset, we find ourselves on the prowl, searching to satisfy some inner, unexplained yearning. Our hunger to be loved causes us to seek out friends. Our desire for acceptance pressures us to perform for the praise of others. We strive for success, driving our minds and bodies harder and farther, hoping that because of our sweat and sacrifice, others will appreciate us more.

But the man or woman who lives only for the love and attention of others is never satisfied – at least not for long. Despite all our efforts, we can never find lasting, fulfilling peace because we have to continually prove our worth to others. Our need to be loved and accepted is merely a symptom of a deeper need – the need that governs our behavior and is the primary source of our emotional pain. Often unrecognized, it is our need for self-worth.

The case of Mark and Beth aptly demonstrates this great need. During their final semester at Cornell University, Mark and Beth fell in love. Beth's eyes sparkled, her walk had that certain lightness, and she found it difficult to concentrate on her studies. As they gazed into each other's eyes, Beth saw the special affection she had always desired. Her need to feel valued and loved was fulfilled through their relationship. Likewise, Mark was encouraged and motivated by Beth's acceptance and admiration of him. With her support, Mark thought he could boldly begin a successful career after graduation.

The summer after they graduated from Cornell, Mark and Beth married, believing their love would provide a permanent sense of self-worth. Unfortunately, Mark and Beth were depending on each other to fill a void that could only be filled by their Creator. Each expected the other always to be loving, accepting, and forgiving, but soon both were disillusioned and even felt betrayed by the other. As the years passed, affirmation turned into sarcasm and ridicule. They had expected each other to consistently provide love and acceptance, but each failure was another brick in their wall of hurt and separation. Recently, Mark and Beth celebrated their 10th wedding anniversary. They had shared ten years of living together, but sadly, very little true, unconditional love. Their search for self-worth and significance ended in despair.

Another example illustrates how the promise of fulfillment through success is an empty promise, often resulting in tragic consequences for ourselves and those around us. Brad and Lisa had been happily married for ten years. Brad was a successful lawyer and Lisa was a homemaker extensively involved in church activities. Their two sons, six-year-old Kyle and eight-year-old David, were well-behaved boys. Although their family appeared perfect to those around them, Brad and Lisa were beginning to experience some real problems. True, Brad's law practice was flourishing, but at the expense of Lisa and the boys. He arrived home later and later each evening and often spent weekends locked in his office. Brad was driven to succeed, believing that satisfaction and contentment were always just one more trial victory away. But each success gave him only temporary fulfillment. Maybe the next one . . . .

He would not allow anything to interfere with his success, not even the needs of his family. At first, Lisa seemed to understand. She knew Brad's work was important, and she hated to protest when he was so busy. Not wanting to burden him, she began to feel guilty for talking to him about family problems. But as weeks turned into months, and Brad remained obsessed by his work, Lisa became resentful. Even though it was painful, she could overlook her own needs, but the boys needed their father. The family never had time to be together anymore, and Brad's promises began sounding hollow. "When this big case is over, the pressure will be off," he'd say, but there was always another case. Brad was continually solving other people's problems, but never those of his own family. Realizing that she and the boys weren't important to Brad, Lisa became bitter and depressed.

As the problems persisted, they became obvious to others. Friends began asking Lisa what was wrong. Finding it difficult at first to admit the situation, Lisa eventually shared her feelings with them. However, she was hurt and surprised by the glib responses from well-intentioned, but insensitive people. "Just trust the Lord," one said. Another close friend advised, "You shouldn't have any problems, Lisa. You're a Christian. With God's help, you can work it out."

Like a fall on a jagged rock, the comments hurt deeply. Lisa began to doubt herself and wonder if she was capable of building a successful marriage and family. Feeling like a failure, she reasoned that perhaps she deserved a broken marriage; perhaps it was her fault and God was punishing her for her sins.

Confused and frustrated, both Brad and Lisa were searching for significance in their own way – Brad in his success as a lawyer and Lisa in her success as a wife and mother. Their lives began to reflect that strange combination of hopelessness and compulsion. Sadly, neither Brad nor Lisa realized that their search should both begin and end with God's Word. In the Scriptures, God supplies the essentials to discover our true significance and worth. The first two chapters of Genesis recount man's creation, revealing man's intended purpose (to honor God) and man's value (that he is a special creation of God). Also, John 10:10 reminds us how much God actually treasures His creation in that Christ came so that man might experience an "abundant life." However, Christians need to realize that this abundant life is lived in a real world filled with pain, rejection, and failure. Therefore, experiencing the abundant life God intended for us does not mean our lives will be problem-free. On the contrary, life itself is simply a series of problems that act as obstacles to our search for significance, and the abundant life is the experience of God's love, forgiveness, and power in the midst of those problems. The Scriptures warn us that we live in the midst of a warfare that can destroy our faith, lower our self-worth, and lead us into depression. In his letter to the Ephesians, Paul instructs us to put on our armor so we can be equipped for spiritual battle. However, it often seems that unsuspecting Christians are the last to know there is a battle going on and that Christ has ultimately won the war. They are surprised and confused by difficulties, thinking that the Christian life is a playground, not a battlefield.

As Christians, our fulfillment in this life depends not on our skills to avoid life's problems, but rather on our ability to apply God's specific solutions to our problems. An accurate understanding of God's truth is the first step in discovering our significance and worth. Unfortunately, many Christians have been exposed to inadequate teaching from both religious and secular sources concerning their self-worth. As a result, Christians today have distorted self-perceptions and are experiencing hopelessness rather than the rich and meaningful life God intended for them.

Christian psychologist Lawrence J. Crabb, Jr., describes our need in this way: "The basic personal need of each person is to regard himself as a worthwhile human being." And, according to William Glasser, "Everyone aspires to have a happy, successful, pleasurable belief in himself."

Whether labeled "self-esteem" or "self-worth," the feeling of significance is crucial to the emotional, spiritual, and social stability of people. The need to believe we are significant is the driving element within the human spirit. Understanding this single need opens the door to understanding our actions and attitudes.

What a waste to attempt to change behavior without truly understanding the driving needs that cause that behavior! Yet, millions of people spend a lifetime searching miserably for love, acceptance, and success without understanding the need that compels them. We must understand that this hunger for self-worth is God-given and can only be satisfied by God. In Genesis, we see that Adam once had a true sense of self-worth gained from those hours he spent walking with God. This was man and his Creator, communing, sharing, and confirming Adam's self-worth through an intimate, personal relationship. Through the eyes of his Heavenly Father, Adam could see that he was deeply loved and fully accepted, with the honor and responsibility of glorifying God. In the same way, our self-worth is not dependent on our ability to earn the acceptance of fickle people, but rather, its true source is the love and acceptance of God. He created us. He alone knows how to fulfill all our needs.

After Adam sinned against God and that special relationship was disrupted, the need for self-confirmation was still present. But since that time, man in his ignorance has foolishly looked to success and the approval of others to fulfill the need that only God can meet.

The purpose of this book is to give clear, Biblical instruction about the basis of your self-worth by helping you:

1)   identify and understand the nature of man's search for significance,

2)   recognize and challenge the inadequate answers, and

3)   apply God's solutions to your search for significance.

In order to fully understand the provisions God has made for our self-worth, we must look back to man's beginning – to the first man and woman and their search for significance.

Author's Note:

With the proliferation of books on both secular and Christian psychology, it is helpful to get some perspective on the Biblical principles taught in The Search For Significance. Some Christian counselors and authors observe the pain caused by low self-esteem, and their solution is to try to inflate the person's ego so he will feel better about himself. Often, there is simply "positive mental attitude" material in Christian lingo.

A few other authors abhor the shallowness of this, "let's all feel good about ourselves", approach, but their reaction takes them to the other extreme. They camp on Christ's teaching that we should hate our lives in order to be His disciples, but they exclude the abundant and clear teaching of Christ's love, forgiveness, and acceptance. This harsh, out-of-balance approach may be stimulating to someone who is very secure in Christ, but it is devastating to most of us.

A healthy, positive self-esteem is not attained by "feel good" superficiality. On the other extreme, a Christ-centered view of ourselves is not detrimental to true discipleship: it is the result of understanding and applying the truths of the Scriptures. Paul wrote, "For through the grace given to me I say to every man among you not to think more highly of himself than he ought to think, but to think so as to have sound judgment." (Romans 12:3) This sound judgment is not based on either pop psychology or spiritual masochism. Sound judgment is based squarely on God's truth. The Search For Significance is designed to clearly present these truths.

Chapter Two

The Origin of the Search

The Old Testament depicts the original incident of sin and the Fall of man:

> *"When the woman saw that the tree was good for food, and that it was a delight to the eyes, and that the tree was desirable to make one wise, she took from its fruit and ate; and she gave also to her husband with her, and he ate; then the eyes of both of them were opened, and they knew that they were naked; and they sewed fig leaves together and made themselves loin coverings" (Genesis 3:6,7).*

To properly understand the devastating effects of this event, we need to examine the nature of man before sin caused him to lose his security and significance. This first created man lived in unclouded, intimate fellowship with God. He was secure and free. In all of God's creation, no creature compared to him. Indeed, Adam was a magnificent creation, complete and perfect in the image of God, designed to reign over all the earth (Genesis 1: 26,27). Adam's purpose was to reflect the glory of God. Through man, God wanted to demonstrate His holiness (Psalm 99: 3-5), love and patience (I Corinthians 13:4), forbearance (I Corinthians 13:7), wisdom (James 3:17), comfort (II Corinthians 1: 3,4), forgiveness (Hebrews 10:17), faithfulness (Psalm 89:1, 2, 5, 8), and grace (Psalm 111:4). Through his intellect, free will, and emotions, man was to be the showcase for God's glorious character.

Obviously, Adam was a very important creation to God. To meet Adam's needs for companionship and understanding, God created a woman and gave her to Adam as his wife. In keeping with their perfect character, God placed Adam and Eve in a perfect environment – a lush, beautiful garden where the Creator Himself provided for their physical needs. Adam and Eve had the challenge and responsibility of supervising this paradise of vegetation and animal life. To satisfy Adam and Eve's spiritual needs, God visited them and talked with them daily. Adam and Eve were perfect in body, mind, and spirit. Like Adam and Eve, Satan himself was created in perfection. At that time, his name was Lucifer, which means "morning star." He was an angel of the highest rank, created to glorify God. He was clothed with beauty and power, and allowed to serve in the presence of God. Sadly, Lucifer's pride caused him to rebel against God, and he was cast from heaven with a third of the angels (Isaiah 14:12-15).

Adam had been given authority over the earth, but if he, too, rebelled against God, he would lose his authority and perfection. He would become a slave of Satan and sin (Romans 6:17) and a child of God's wrath (Ephesians 2:3). Therefore, destroying man was Satan's way to reign on earth and, he thought, thwart the plan of God.

To accomplish his goal, Satan began by deceiving Eve, who fell to the temptation. Eve ate of the tree of the knowledge of good and evil, believing it would make her wiser and like God. Adam, however, was not deceived. He deliberately chose to forsake the love and security of God and follow Eve in sin. Paul explained this fact to Timothy:

"And it was not Adam who was deceived, but the woman being quite deceived, fell into transgression" (I Timothy 2:14).

In doing this, Adam not only lost the glory God had intended for mankind, but he also forfeited his close communion and fellowship with God. Also, Adam's deliberate rebellion aided Satan's purpose, giving him power and authority on earth.

Even though Adam lost his dominion over the earth, God did not lose him as His image bearer. Even in the moment of judgment, God told of His love to forgive sin and restore man to a powerful and intimate relationship with Him. From that moment on, all history led to a single hill outside Jerusalem where God appointed a Savior to pay the penalty for our sin of rebellion.

Though we justly deserve the wrath of God because of our deliberate rebellion (our attempts to find security and purpose apart from God), His Son became our substitute, experienced the wrath our rebellion deserves, and paid the penalty for our sins. Christ's death is the most overwhelming evidence of God's love for us. Because of this, our relationship with God is restored and we are able to partake of His nature and character, able once again to commune with Him and able to reflect His love to all the world.

Spread the good news! Man is not lost forever. God has not given up on us. He has bought us out of slavery to sin by the payment of Christ's death on the cross. Satan's rule can be broken and we can reign with Christ. We can be restored to the security and significance for which we have been created – not simply in eternity, but here and now as well.

We must never forget that God wants His children to bear His image and to rule with Him. Adam's sin has had tragic consequences, but through God's plan of redemption, we can still have the unspeakable privilege of relating to Him. God has provided the solution, but the question is this: Will we accept Christ's death as the payment for our sins and discover the powerful implications of our salvation, or will we continue to follow Satan's lies and deception?

Perhaps you need to deal conclusively with this choice here and now. We cannot pay for our sins, but Christ did it for us as a free gift. Paul wrote to the Ephesian Christians:

> *"For by grace (unmerited favor) you have been saved (rescued from spiritual death – hell) through faith (trust); and that not of yourselves, it is the gift of God; not as a result of works, that no one should boast" (Ephesians 2:8,9).*

Are you trusting in your own abilities to earn acceptance with God, or are you trusting in the death of Christ to pay for your sins and the resurrection of Christ to give you new life? Take a moment to reflect on this question: On a scale of 0-100%, how sure are you that you would spend eternity with God if you died today? An answer of less than 100% may indicate that you are trusting, at least in part, in yourself. You may be thinking, "Isn't that arrogant to say you are 100% sure?" Indeed, it would be arrogance if you were trusting in yourself – your abilities, your actions and good deeds – to earn your salvation. However, if you are no longer trusting your own efforts but are trusting in the all-sufficient payment of Christ, then 100% certainty is a response of humility and thankfulness.

Reflect on a second question: If you were to die today and stand before God, and He were to ask you, "Why should I let you into heaven?", what would you tell Him? Would you mention your abilities, church attendance, kindness to others, Christian service, abstinence from some particular sin, or some other good deeds? Paul writes to Titus:

> *"But when the kindness of God our Savior and His love for mankind appeared, He saved us, not on the basis of*

*deeds which we have done in righteousness, but according to
His mercy..." (Titus 3:4,5).*

We must give up our own efforts to achieve righteousness and
believe that Christ's death and resurrection alone are sufficient to pay
for our sin and separation from God.

Perhaps you have intellectually believed that Jesus Christ lived
2000 years ago, performed miracles, died on the cross, and was raised
from the dead. Perhaps you have even felt close to God at times in
your life. But Biblical faith is more than intellectual assent or warm
emotions. Consider the analogy of a wedding. An engaged couple may
intellectually know they want to marry each other, and they probably
feel very close to one another, but until they willfully say, "I do," to
each other, they are not married. Many people are at this point in
their relationship with Christ. They need to say, "I do," to Him.

If there is any question about whether you have conclusively accepted Christ's substitutionary death to pay for the wrath you deserve
for your sins, take some time to think about the two questions we have
examined, and reflect on His love and forgiveness. Then, respond by
trusting in Christ and accepting His payment for your sins. You can
use this prayer to express your faith:

Lord Jesus, I need You. I want You to be my Savior and Lord. I
accept Your death on the cross as the complete payment for my sins.
Thank You for forgiving me and giving me new life. Help me to grow
in my understanding of Your love and power so that my life will bring
honor to You. Amen.

The moment you trust Christ, many wonderful things happen to
you:

All your sins are forgiven: past, present, and future (Colossians
2:13,14).
You become a child of God (John 1:12, Romans 8:15).

You receive eternal life (John 5:24).

You are delivered from Satan's domain and transferred into the kingdom of Christ (Colossians 1:13).

Christ comes to dwell within you (Colossians 1:27, Revelation 3:20).

You become a new creation (II Corinthians 5:17).

You are declared righteous by God (II Corinthians 5:21).

You enter into a love relationship with God (I John 4:9-11).

You are accepted by God (Colossians 1:19-22).

Thank God for His wonderful grace and experience *"the love of Christ which surpasses knowledge"* (Ephesians 3:19). You may want to use the rest of this page to write a letter to God expressing your gratitude to Him.

Chapter Three

The Saving Solution vs. Satan's Snare

Separated from his Creator and the magnificent position he was intended to enjoy, Adam's mind became darkened and ignorant (Ephesians 4:17-19). Before the Fall, his mind had been an extraordinary example of reasoning and wisdom. However, after the Fall, Adam's mind was filled with vain imaginations and limited by a lack of intimate communication with God.

Notice how Satan snared Eve. He told her:

> *"For God knows that in the day you eat from it your eyes will be opened, and you will be like God, knowing good and evil" (Genesis 3:5).*

Here, Satan directly questioned God's truthfulness, implying that Eve could have greater significance apart from God and that eating the forbidden fruit would reveal hidden knowledge and would make her know good from evil like God Himself.

How subtly Satan twisted God's truth into history's most believed lie! The God of love said to Adam, "You are My image bearer, My companion ruler, the reflection of My glory," but Satan distorted the message to say, "You are something other than that, something more. Eat the fruit and you'll find out!"

Being deceived, Eve traded the truth of God for the lie of the serpent. She ate the forbidden fruit. Then Adam followed her in sinful rebellion against God, and he too, ate forbidden fruit. One of the tragic implications of this event is that mankind lost his secure status with God and began to struggle with feelings of arrogance, inadequacy, and despair, valuing the opinions of others more than the truth of God. This has robbed man of his true self-worth and has put him on a continual, but fruitless, search for significance through his success and the approval of others.

In one form or another, Satan's lie still thrives today. For example, humanism, the central philosophy of our schools and society, teaches that man is above all else, that he alone is the center of meaning.   Teaching that man has meaning totally apart from God, humanism leaves morality, justice, and behavior to the discretion of "enlightened" man and encourages people to worship man and nature rather than God. Living without God's divine truth, humanity sinks lower and lower in depravity, blindly following a philosophy that intends to heighten the dignity of man, but instead lowers us to the level of animals. Rather than spiritual and emotional people, we have been classified as merely natural phenomena of time plus chance, no different than rocks, animals, or clouds. The apostle Paul described this foolish and demeaning perspective of man in Romans 1:20-25:

> "For since the creation of the world His invisible attributes, His eternal power and divine nature, have been clearly seen, being understood through what has been made, so that they are without excuse. For even though they knew God, they did not honor Him as God, or give thanks; but they became futile in their speculations, and their foolish heart was darkened. Professing to be wise, they became

*fools, and exchanged the glory of the incorruptible God for
an image in the form of corruptible man and of birds and
four-footed animals and crawling creatures. Therefore God
gave them over in the lusts of their hearts to impurity, that
their bodies might be dishonored among them. For they exchanged the truth of God for a lie, and worshiped and served
the creature rather than the Creator, who is blessed forever.
Amen."*

In the beginning, God declared that man was created to reign
with Him; however, man rejected God's truth and chose instead to
believe Satan's lie. Today, man continues to reject God's truth and
offer of salvation through Jesus Christ. He chooses instead to trust in
his success and the opinions of others to give him a sense of self-
worth, though the Scriptures clearly teach that man apart from Christ
is enslaved to sin and condemned to an eternity in hell.

After the Fall, man has failed to turn to God for the truth about
himself. Instead he has looked to others to meet his inescapable
need for self-worth. "I am what others say I am," he has reasoned. "I
will find my value in their opinions of me." Isn't it amazing that we
turn to others who have a perspective as limited and darkened as our
own to discover our worth! Rather than relying on God's steady, uplift-
ing reassurance of who we are, we turn to others who judge our worth
by our ability to meet their standards.

Because our performance and our ability to please others so
dominates our search for significance, we have difficulty recognizing
the distinction between our real identity and the way we behave, a
realization crucial to understanding our true worth. Our true worth is
not based on our behavior or the approval of others. It is based on
what God's Word says is true of us. Our behavior, then, is a reflection
of our beliefs about who we are. Our behavior is consistent with what
we think to be true about ourselves (Proverbs 23:7). If we base our
worth solidly on the truths of God's Word, our behavior will reflect

His love, grace and power. But if we base our worth on our abilities or the fickle approval of others, our behavior will reflect the insecurity, fear, and anger that comes from that unstable base.

My dog, Whitey, fritters away time sleeping. When he isn't sleeping, he's busy barking at strangers and scratching at fleas. It is behavior I've come to expect from my pet. But suppose you and I decide to behave like my dog. Suppose we started spending our time sleeping, crawling around on our hands and knees, barking at strangers and passing cars. Suddenly we begin performing like my dog, but that behavior does not make us dogs! The way we behave is only an expression of the beliefs we hold about ourselves, not an indication of our true worth. Therefore, we cannot experience a permanent change in our behavior without first changing what we believe about ourselves.

This truth is evident in the case of Scott. Scott grew up in a home without praise, being discouraged by his parents whenever he attempted anything new and challenging. After twenty years of hearing, "You'll never be able to do anything, Scott, so don't even try," he believed it himself. Neither Scott nor his parents could now understand why he flunked out of college and continually shuffled from one job to another, never able to achieve success. Believing he was doing the best he could do but knowing he would always fail, Scott consistently performed according to his self-perception.

Separated from God and His Word, people have only their abilities and the opinions of others on which to base their worth, and the circumstances around them will ultimately control the way they feel about themselves.

Take the case of Stacy, a young girl who became pregnant when she was just seventeen. Stacy gave her baby up for adoption, and only her family knew of the incident. Several years later, Stacy fell in love with and married a loving man named Ron. Fearing his reaction, she never told Ron about the baby. Over the years, Stacy concealed her guilt and grief until finally, the pressure became too overwhelming and she admitted the entire episode to Ron.

Surprisingly, Ron did not respond in anger. He understood the agony she had carried for so many years and loved her in spite of her past. However, it was Stacy who at this point could not cope. Unable to accept Ron's forgiveness and knowing she had failed according to society's standards, Stacy felt unworthy of Ron's love. Stacy could not forgive herself and chose to leave her husband.

In this case, Stacy fell victim to one of Satan's most effective lies: "Those who fail are unworthy of love and deserve to be blamed and condemned." Because she failed in her own eyes, Stacy's perception of herself was affected. Each of us has probably failed badly at some point in our lives. Perhaps some particular sin or weakness has caused us to feel condemned and unworthy of love. Our opinion of ourselves, as well as our method of evaluating others, comes from a mind limited by a veil of sin (II Corinthians 3:14). Therefore, our evaluation of ourselves will inevitably lead to despair.

In spite of Adam and Eve's sin, God's plan was to bring man back to the destiny for which he had been originally created – to bear His image. To accomplish this, God gives a new nature to all who will believe in Christ. This new nature is able to reflect God's character and rule His creation. In Luke 10:19 Jesus spoke of the authority of this new nature when He said,

> *"Behold, I have given you authority to tread upon serpents and scorpions and over all the power of the enemy, and nothing shall injure you."*

However, Satan continues to deceive people, including many Christians, to believe that the basis of their worth is their performance and their ability to please others. This equation reflects Satan's lie:

SELF-WORTH = PERFORMANCE + OTHERS' OPINION

Can we overcome Satan's deception and reject this basis of our self-worth? Can we trust God's complete acceptance of us as His sons and daughters and allow Him to free us from this dependency on success and others' approval? Rejecting Satan's lie and accepting God's evaluation of us leads to a renewed hope, joy, and purpose in life.

We all have compelling needs for love, acceptance, and purpose, and we will go to virtually any lengths to have those needs met. Many of us have become masters at "playing the game" to be successful and win the approval of others. Others, however, have failed often enough and experienced the pain of disapproval often enough that they have given up, withdrawing into a shell of hurt, numbness, or depression. Both kinds of people live by the deception that their worth is based on their performance and others' opinions – some of us are simply more adept than others at playing that game.

Our attempts to meet our needs for success and approval fall into two broad categories: compulsiveness and withdrawal. Some people put out extra effort, work extra hours, and try to say just the right thing so they will be successful and please those around them. These people may have a compelling desire to be in control of every situation. They are perfectionists. If a job isn't done to perfection, if they aren't dressed just right, if they aren't considered "the best" by their peers, then they work harder until they achieve that coveted status. And woe to the poor soul who gets in the way! Whoever doesn't contribute to their success and acclaim is a threat to their self-esteem – an unacceptable threat. They may be very personable and have a lot of "friends," but the goal of these relationships may not be to give encouragement and love; it may be to manipulate others to contribute to their success. That may sound harsh, but people who are driven to succeed use practically everything and everybody to meet that need.

The other broad category is withdrawal. These people try to avoid failure and disapproval by avoiding risks. They don't volunteer for the jobs that have much risk of failure. They gravitate toward people who are comforting and kind, avoiding relationships that might demand vulnerability, and consequently the pain of rejection. They may appear to be easy-going, but inside they are running from every potential situation or relationship that might not succeed.

Obviously these are two broad categories. Most of us are some combination of the two, willing to take risks and work hard in the areas where we are likely to succeed, but avoiding the people and situations where rejection and failure are likely.

For three years Rob and Kathy had dated. Kathy was a perfectionist. Her clothes, her hair, her work, her car...and her boyfriend had to be just right. Rob was a good-natured, fun-loving fellow who was not so concerned about every detail of life. Predictably, the more intense Kathy became about having everything and everybody "just right," the more passive and easy-going Rob became. The spiral of intensity and passivity kept going until it hit rock bottom. As they sat in my office, Kathy quickly saw that her perfectionism came from a misplaced base of security: her performance instead of Christ. But Rob said he didn't have a problem with performance. He certainly didn't have a compelling drive to succeed, and he didn't pressure people around him to "get their act together." In the midst of these explanations, I asked, "But wait, Rob, what about your tendency to withdraw? Why do you think you do that?" It still didn't compute. Finally, after several hours he saw it. He based his security on his performance just as much as Kathy did, but he handled it differently. She became more compulsive to have things "just right," while he withdrew to avoid failure. Both of them recognized the root of the problem and started believing that their worth is secure in Christ. Today, Kathy is less intense about her performance, and Rob doesn't run from failure as much as he used to. They are learning to be intense about the right things: Christ and His kingdom.

When we base our security on success and others' opinions, we become dependent on our ability to perform and our ability to please others. We develop a "have to" mentality: "I have to do well on this exam (or my security as a 'good student' will be threatened);" "I have to make that deal (or it will mean that my boss will think I am a failure);" "My father (or mother, spouse, or friend) has to appreciate me and be happy with my decisions (because I cannot cope with his disapproval)." Isn't it odd that we tend to base our self-worth on how well we perform and please others instead of what the Sovereign God of the Universe, our all-wise, omniscient Savior says is true of us?

We do not "have to" be successful or "have to" be pleasing to others to have healthy self-esteem and worth. That worth has freely and conclusively been given to us by God. Failure or the disapproval of others can't take it away! Therefore, a person can conclude, "It would be nice to be approved by my parents (or whomever), but if they don't approve of me, I'm still loved and accepted by God." Do you see the difference? The "have to" mentality is sheer slavery to performance and the opinions of others, but we are secure and free in Christ. We don't "have to" have success or anyone else's approval. Of course, "it would be nice to have" success and their approval, but the point is clear: Christ is the source of our security; Christ is the basis of our worth; Christ is the only One who promises and never fails.

This book is dedicated to understanding, applying, and experiencing the foundational truths of God's Word. In the remaining chapters, we will identify four specific false beliefs of Satan's deception. In addition, we will discover God's gracious, effective, and permanent solution to our search for significance.

INTRODUCTION TO CHAPTERS 4, 5, 6, & 7

Often it is helpful to see a general outline when attempting to grasp new concepts. In the next four chapters, we will examine the four false beliefs resulting from Satan's deception and the inescapable consequences that accompany these beliefs. Finally, we will examine God's specific solution, accompanied by some practical exercises. Here is an overview of the next four chapters:

Chapter 4: The Performance Trap

False Belief

> *I must meet certain standards to feel good about myself.*

Consequences of the False Belief
> The Fear of Failure

God's Answer: Justification

Justification means God not only has forgiven me of my sins, but also has granted me the righteousness of Christ. Because of justification, I have the righteousness of Christ and am pleasing to the Father (Romans 5:1).

Chapter 5: Approval Addict

False Belief

> *I must be approved (accepted) by certain others to feel good about myself.*

Consequences of the False Belief
> The Fear of Rejection

God's Answer: Reconciliation

Reconciliation means that although at one time I was hostile and alienated from God, I now have been forgiven and brought into an intimate relationship with God. Consequently, I am totally accepted by God (Colossians 1:21,22).

Chapter 6: The Blame Game

False Belief

> *Those who fail are unworthy of love and deserve to be punished.*

Consequences of the False Belief

The Fear of Punishment/Punishing Others

God's Answer: Propitiation

Propitiation means Christ satisfied the wrath of God by His death on the cross; therefore I am deeply loved by God (I John 4:9-11).

Chapter 7: Shame

False Belief

> *I am what I am. I cannot change. I am hopeless.*

Consequences of the False Belief

Shame, Inferiority, Habitually Destructive Behavior Patterns

God's Answer: Regeneration

Regeneration means that I am a new creation in Christ (John 3:3-6).

Chapter Four

The Performance Trap

Most of us are unaware how thoroughly Satan has deceived us. He has led us blindly down a path of destruction, captives of our inability to consistently meet our standards and slaves of low self-esteem. Satan has shackled us in chains that keep us from experiencing the love, freedom, and purposes of Christ.

In Colossians 2:8, Paul warns:

> *"See to it that no one takes you captive through philosophy and empty deception, according to the tradition of men, according to the elementary principles of the world, rather than according to Christ."*

Indeed, we've reached a true mark of maturity when we begin testing the deceitful thoughts of our minds against the Word of God. We no longer have to live by our fleshly thoughts; we have the mind of Christ (I Corinthians 2:16). Through His Spirit, we can challenge the indoctrinations and traditions that have long held us in guilt and condemnation. Then we can replace those deceptions with the powerful truths of the Scriptures.

One of the main deceptions we tend to believe is that success will bring fulfillment and happiness. Again and again, we've tried to measure up, thinking that if we could meet certain standards, we would feel good about ourselves. But again and again, we've failed and are left feeling miserable. Even if we succeed almost all of the time, occasional failure can be so devastating that it can dominate our perception of ourselves.

Consciously or unconsciously, all of us have experienced this feeling that we must meet certain arbitrary standards to attain self-worth. At that point, we are accepting the first false belief: *"I must meet certain standards in order to feel good about myself."* When we believe this about ourselves, Satan's distortion of truth is reflected in our attitudes and behavior.

Because of our unique personalities, we react very differently to this deception. As we saw in the last chapter, one frequent response is that people become slaves to perfectionism – driving themselves incessantly toward attaining goals. Perfectionists can be quite vulnerable to serious mood disorders, and they often anticipate rejection when they believe they haven't met the standards they are trying so hard to meet. Therefore, perfectionists tend to react defensively to criticism and demand to be in control of most situations they encounter. Because they are more competent than most, perfectionists see nothing wrong with their compulsions. "I just like to see things done well," they claim. There is certainly nothing inherently wrong with doing things well, but the problem is that perfectionists base their self-worth on their ability to accomplish a goal. Therefore, failure is a threat and is totally unacceptable to them.

Karen, a wife, mother, and civic leader, seemed ideal to everyone who knew her. She was a perfectionist. Her house looked picture-perfect, her kids were always spotless, and her skills as president of the Ladies' Auxiliary were superb. In all areas, Karen was always in charge, always successful.

However, one step out of the pattern Karen had set could lead to a tremendous uproar. When others failed to comply with her every demand, her condemnation was quick and cruel. One day, Karen's husband, Jerry, could stand no more. He wanted an understanding wife, someone he could talk to and share with, not an ego-centric, self-driven perfectionist. Friends simply could not understand why Jerry chose to leave such a seemingly perfect wife.

Like Karen, many people who are high achievers, are driven beyond healthy limitations. Rarely relaxing and enjoying life, they let their families and relationships suffer as they strive to accomplish their often unrealistic goals.

On the other hand, the same false belief *("I must meet certain standards to feel good about myself")* that drives many to perfectionism, sends still others into a tailspin of despair. They never expect to achieve anything or feel good about themselves. Because of their past failures, they are quick to interpret present failures as an accurate reflection of their worthlessness. Fearing additional failures, they become despondent and quit trying.

Finally, another significant problem often results from the pressure of having to meet self-imposed standards in order to feel good about ourselves: a rules-dominated life. Individuals caught in this trap have a set of rules for every situation in life and continually place their attention on their performance and ability to adhere to their schedule. For example, Brent made a list every day of what he could accomplish if everything went perfectly. He was always a little tense because he needed to use every moment effectively to reach his goals. If things didn't go well or if somebody took up too much of his time, Brent got angry. Efficient, effective use of time was his way of attaining fulfillment, but he was miserable. He was constantly driven to do more, but his best was never enough to satisfy him. Brent failed to realize that the focus of the Christian life should be on Christ, not on self-imposed regulations. Our experience of Christ's lordship is dependent on our attending to His instruction moment by moment, not our own regimented schedule.

As these cases demonstrate, the first false belief: "*I must meet certain standards in order to feel good about myself,*" results in a fear of failure. How affected are you by this belief? Take the following test to determine how strongly you fear failure.

FEAR OF FAILURE TEST

Read the following statements. Look at the top of the test and choose the term which best describes your response. Put the number above that term in the blank beside the statement.

1	2	3	4	5	6	7
Always	Very Often	Often	Sometimes	Seldom	Very Seldom	Never

_____1. Because of fear, I often avoid participating in certain activities.

_____2. When I sense I might experience failure in some important area, I become nervous and anxious.

_____3. I worry.

_____4. I have unexplained anxiety.

_____5. I am a perfectionist.

_____6. I am compelled to justify my mistakes.

_____7. There are certain areas in which I feel I must succeed.

_____8. I become depressed when I fail.

_____ 9.   I become angry with people who interfere with my atempts to succeed, and as a result, make me appear incompetent.

_____ 10.   I am self-critical.

_____   Total (Add up the numbers you have placed in the blanks.)

INTERPRETATION OF SCORE

If your score is...

57-70
God apparently has released you from the fear of failure that plagues most people. The major exceptions to this are those who are either greatly deceived or have become callous to their own emotions as a way to suppress the pain.

47-56
The fear of failure rarely or only in certain situations controls your experiences. Again, the only major exception involves those who are not honest with themselves.

37-46
When you experience emotional problems, they may relate to a sense of failure or some form of criticism. In looking back, you can probably relate many of your decisions to this fear. Many of your decisions in the future will also be affected by the fear of failure unless you take direct action to overcome it.

27-36
Not only is the above category true of your experiences, but this fear of failure forms a general backdrop to your life. There are probably few days that you are not affected in some way by the fear of failure. Unfortunately, this also robs you of the joy and peace your salvation was meant to bring.

0-26

Experiences of failure dominate your memory and have probably resulted in a great deal of depression. These problems will remain until some definitive action is taken. In other words, this condition will not simply disappear; time alone cannot heal your pain. You must deal with the root issue.

THE EFFECTS OF THE FEAR OF FAILURE

As long as we operate according to Satan's plan, we are susceptible to the fear of failure. Our personal experience of this fear is determined by the difference between our performance standards and our ability to meet those standards.

Although we experience the fear of failure, we must also remember that God wants us to be free from this fear so that we will be able to honor Him more and more. For our benefit, He allows circumstances in our lives to enable us to recognize our blind adherence to Satan's deceptions. Many times, these circumstances seem very negative, but through them, we can learn valuable, life-changing truths. In Psalm 107:33-36, we see a poetic example of this:

> *"He changes rivers into a wilderness, And springs of water into a thirsty ground; A fruitful land into a salt waste, Because of the wickedness of those who dwell in it. He changes a wilderness into a pool of water, and a dry land into springs of water; And there He makes the hungry to dwell, So that they may establish an inhabited city."*

Has your fruitful land become a salt waste? Maybe God is trying to get your attention to teach you a tremendously important lesson: that success or failure is not the basis of your self-worth. Maybe the only way you would learn that lesson is by experiencing the pain of failure. In His great love, God leads us through experiences that are difficult, but essential to our growth and development.

The fear of failure can affect our lives in many ways. The following list is not an exhaustive discussion of these problems, nor are all these problems explained completely by the fear of failure. However, recognizing and removing the fear of failure in each of these situations could result in dramatic changes.

Perfectionism

One of the most common symptoms of the fear of failure is perfectionism: an unwillingness to fail. This tendency suffocates joy and creativity, and because any failure is a threat, it focuses our attention on the one thing that failed rather than the ten things that went well. A few areas where people tend to be perfectionists include: doing work well, being punctual, cleaning the house or car, their appearance, some skill, or practically anything we could name! These people usually appear to be highly motivated, but their motivations come from the fact that they are trying desperately not to lose self-esteem because of failure.

Avoiding Risks

Another very common result of the fear of failure is that people are willing to be involved in activities only if they can do them well. They avoid new and challenging activities because the risk of failure is too great. Avoiding risks may seem comfortable to them, but it severely limits the scope of creativity and self-expression, and also, it limits the scope of their service to God.

Anger, Resentment

When injured or insulted by others, we often become angry. This anger can easily develop into resentment – a deep bitterness toward the offender. Such resentment is often associated with our fear of failure. For example, when confronted by others about our performance, we may be defensive and retaliate with anger and resentment.

It is important to realize that the relief provided by our retaliation is short-lived, if indeed there is any relief at all.

Anxiety and Fear

Failure often is the source of both self-condemnation and the disapproval of others, both of which are severe blows to a self-worth based on personal success and approval. The obvious result is anxiety. If failure is great enough or occurs often enough, it can harden into a negative self-concept in which the person expects to fail at virtually every endeavor. This negative self-concept perpetuates itself and leads to a downward spiral of failure and despair.

Pride

When a person bases his self-worth on his performance and is successful, it leads to an inflated view of himself: pride. A few people persist in this self-exaltation through any and all circumstances; for most of us, however, this sense of self-esteem lasts only until our next failure (or risk of failure). The self-confidence that most of us try to portray is only a facade to hide our fear of failure and insecurity.

Schizophrenia

Schizophrenia, which could be called the "Hider's Disease," is a condition in which people try to escape the pain of failure and rejection by creating their own separate world. Strong elements of rejection that are related to schizophrenia will be discussed in a following section.

Depression

Experiencing failure and fearing subsequent failure can lead people into deep depression. Once depressed, many people become passive in their actions, believing there is no hope for change. On the other hand, a depressed person may also experience intense anger concerning his failures. Depression is the body's means of blocking psychological pain by numbing physical and emotional functions.

Chemical Dependency

Many people attempt to ease the pain and fear of failure by using drugs or alcohol. Although the chemicals are supposed to remove the pressure to perform, the pleasure of the moment is quickly followed by the despair of realizing an inability to cope without the chemical. This pain-pleasure cycle continues, slowly draining the life out of its victim.

Users of cocaine, a currently popular drug, provide a clear example of this condition. A major reason for cocaine's popularity is its ability to produce feelings of greater self-esteem. However, it is interesting that generally, only successful people can afford the drug. Therefore, if success truly provided a sense of self-esteem, these people would not be in the market for the drug in the first place.

Dishonesty

Dishonesty is an attempt to hide a person's failure, but it seldom blunts the pain. Few of us tell blatant lies, but many of us are dishonest in a more subtle way: exaggerating the truth so good things will seem a little better or bad things will seem a little worse. Exaggerating the truth is another way we try to hide our failures or impress others.

Low Motivation

Much of what is known as low motivation or laziness can be better understood as hopelessness. If people believe they will fail, then they will have no reason to exert any effort. The pain they endure for their passivity seems relatively minor and acceptable compared to the more intense pain of genuinely trying and failing.

Sexual Dysfunction

The emotional trauma caused by failure can cause disturbances in sexual activity. Then, rather than experiencing the pain of failing sexually, many tend to avoid sex altogether.

The more sensitive you become to the fear of failure and the problems it may cause, the more you will understand your own behavior as well as the behavior of others.

GOD'S ANSWER: JUSTIFICATION

If we base our self-worth on our ability to meet standards, we will try to compensate by either avoiding risks or trying to succeed no matter what the cost. Either way, failure looms as a constant enemy. But God has set us free from the fear of failure! He has given us a secure self-worth totally apart from our ability to perform. We have been justified, placed in right standing before God through Christ's death on the cross to pay for our sins. But God didn't stop with our forgiveness; He also granted us the very righteousness of Christ (II Corinthians 5:21)!

Visualize two ledgers. On one ledger is a list of all of your sins. On the other ledger is a list of the righteousness of Christ. Now exchange your ledger for Christ's. This exemplifies justification – transferring our sin to Christ and His righteousness to us. II Corinthians 5:21 says:

"He made Him (Christ) who knew no sin to become sin on our behalf, that we might become the righteousness of God in Him."

Once I heard a radio preacher berate his congregation for their hidden sins. He exclaimed, "Don't you know that someday you're going to die and God is going to flash all your sins upon a giant screen in heaven for all the world to see?" How tragically this minister misunderstood God's gracious gift of justification! Justification carries no guilt with it, and it has no memory of past transgressions. Christ paid for all our sins at the cross – past, present, and future. Hebrews 10:17 says, "*And their sins and their lawless deeds I will remember no more.*" We are completely forgiven by God!

As marvelous as it is, justification means more than forgiveness of sins. In the same act of love through which God forgave our sin, He also provided our righteousness. Righteousness is the worthiness to stand in God's presence without fear of condemnation. Now we can stand in God's presence, for at the moment God forgave our many sins, He also credited to us the very righteousness of Christ.

By imputing righteousness to us, God attributes Christ's worth to us. The moment we accept Christ, God no longer sees us as condemned sinners. Instead, we are forgiven and Christ's righteousness is granted to us, and God sees us as completely righteous and in right standing with Him. Therefore, we are fully pleasing to Him.

God intended that Adam and his descendants be righteous people, experiencing His love and eternal purposes, but sin short-circuited that relationship. God's perfect payment for sin satisfies the righteous wrath of God, and enables us to again have that status of righteousness and to delight in knowing and honoring the Lord. God desires those of us who have been redeemed to experience the realities of His redemption. We are forgiven and righteous because of Christ's sacrifice; therefore, we are pleasing to God in spite of our failures. That reality replaces the fear of failure with peace, hope, and joy. Even great successes do not bring lasting happiness, and failure need not be a millstone around our necks. Neither success nor failure is the proper basis of our self-worth. Christ alone is the source of forgiveness, freedom, joy, and purpose.

At this point, it would be typical for many people to become uneasy, believing the gravity of sin is being overlooked in these statements. As you will see, I am not minimizing the destructiveness of sin. I am simply trying to elevate our view of the results of Christ's payment on the cross. Understanding our complete forgiveness and acceptance before God does not promote a casual attitude toward sin. Quite the contrary, it gives us a greater desire to live for and serve the One who died to free us from sin (II Corinthians 5:14,15; I Corinthians 6:19,20). Let's look at some strong reasons to obey and serve God with joy.

REASONS FOR OBEDIENCE

The love of God and His acceptance of us is based on grace, His unmerited favor. It is not based on our ability to impress God through our good deeds. But if we are accepted on the basis of His grace and not our deeds, why should we obey God? Here are five compelling reasons to obey Him:

Love Constrains

The Christians at Corinth must have posed these same questions to Paul. He responded that the love of Christ motivates us to live for Him. Christ's death revealed the depth of His love for us. Our obedience reveals the depth of our love for Him.

> "For the love of Christ constrains us, having concluded this, that one died for all...and He died for all that they who live should no longer live for themselves, but for Him who died and rose again on their behalf" (II Corinthians 5:14,15).

Notice the word "concluded" in this passage. This word means to analyze an issue and determine its meaning and value. In other words, Paul says that those who comprehend Christ's sacrifice on the cross are compelled by its immeasurable value to live not for themselves, but for Him who made the sacrifice.

True love for Christ is a response to His love for us. As we experience His love, we find our hearts overflowing with love for Him.

Christ offers us divine healing and unconditional love. His love is not based on our performance or ability, and it never condemns. Look again. The Bible does not state that the love of Christ "might constrain." It simply says it "constrains." Therefore, when we find ourselves in rebellion against God, it is a good indication that we have been deceived about some aspect of the love of Christ.

Discipline From The Father

Because He truly loves us, our Heavenly Father has given us the Holy Spirit to convict us of our sin. This conviction is proof that we have become the sons of God (Hebrews 12:5-11). Although He reproves us in love when we disobey, God never punishes us in anger because Christ took the wrath we deserve for our sins once and for all.

If this is true, when does the Lord discipline us? Generally, God does not discipline us each time we do wrong, but only when we persist in wrongdoing. If we were quick to recognize a wrong and correct it, God would have no need to discipline us. But we must realize that when discipline does come, it is sent for correction, not condemnation. Paul wrote:

> "But when we are judged, we are disciplined by the Lord
> in order that we may not be condemned along with the
> world" (I Corinthians 11:32).

Another reason God disciplines us is to protect us from the painful effects of sin. Just as parents use discipline to teach their children that certain activities are harmful to them, our Heavenly Father disciplines us to get our attention so He can teach us that sin is harmful to us. Whether for correction or protection, God's motive for discipline is always love, never anger or revenge. The realization that His discipline is always for our good makes us more open to learn the lessons He wants us to learn.

Sin Is Destructive

The most common responses to sin in our society are laughter and tolerance. Even many Christians seem to think that sin is "no big deal." We need to have our eyes opened to the obvious facts around us about the tremendous destructiveness of sin. Broken homes, hatred, bitterness, suicide, alcohol and drug abuse, sleeplessness, tension, and many other symptoms of sin are rampant.

When we sin, we grieve the Holy Spirit and block His power in our lives. As a result, we are left to our own abilities to combat the conforming pressures of the world. If we truly believed in the destructiveness of sin, we would be quite afraid of it. However, we are deceived because sin is pleasurable – at least temporarily. In the end, sin will bite like a serpent and sting like an adder (Proverbs 23:32). The man who sows evil will reap evil (Galatians 6:7), and the man who willingly and continually sins will destroy himself. Knowing this, we should trust God's infinite wisdom by believing that He has not lied to us concerning the ultimately painful effects of sin.

Eternal Rewards

Yet another compelling reason to live for the glory of God is the fact that we will be rewarded in heaven for our service to God. Two passages clearly illustrate this fact:

> "For we must all appear before the judgment seat of Christ, that each one may be recompensed for his deeds in the body, according to what he has done, whether good or bad" (II Corinthians 5:10).

"Now if any man builds upon the foundation with gold, silver, precious stones, wood, hay, straw, each man's work will become evident; for the day will show it, because it is to be revealed with fire; and the fire itself will test the quality of each man's work. If any man's work which he has built upon it remains, he shall receive a reward. If any man's work is burned up, he shall suffer loss; but he himself shall be saved, yet so as through fire" (I Corinthians 3:12-15).

Through Christ's payment for us on the cross, we have escaped eternal judgment; however, our actions will be judged at the judgment seat of Christ. Here our performance will be evaluated, and rewards will be presented for service to God. Rewards shall be given to those whose deeds were done to honor Christ, but those deeds done for any other motives will be consumed by fire. Performance that reflects a desire to honor Christ will receive rewards and commendation, but performance that is an attempt to earn God's acceptance, earn the approval of others, or meet our own standards will be rejected by God.

Christ Is Worthy

Our most noble motivation for serving Christ is simply that He is worthy of our love and obedience:

"After these things I looked, and behold, a door standing open in heaven, and the first voice which I had heard, like the sound of a trumpet speaking with me, said, 'Come up here, and I will show you what must take place after these things.' Immediately I was in the Spirit; and behold, a throne was standing in heaven, and One sitting on the throne. And He who was sitting was like a jasper stone and a sardius in appearance; and there was a rainbow around the throne, like an emerald in appearance. And around the throne were twen-

ty-four thrones; and upon the thrones I saw twenty-four elders sitting, clothed in white garments, and golden crowns on their heads. . . .

"And when the living creatures give glory and honor and thanks to Him who sits on the throne, to Him who lives forever and ever, the twenty-four elders will fall down before Him who sits on the throne, and will worship Him who lives forever and ever, and will cast their crowns before the throne, saying, 'Worthy, art thou, our Lord and our God, to receive glory and honor and power; for Thou didst create all things, and because of Thy will they existed, and were created'" (Revelation 4:1-4, 9-11).

Christ is worthy of our affection and obedience. There is no other person, no goal, no fame or status, and no material possession that can compare to Christ. The more we understand His love and majesty, the more we will praise Him and desire that He be honored at the expense of everything else. Our hearts will reflect the psalmist's perspective:

"Whom have I in heaven but Thee? And besides Thee I desire nothing on earth. . . . But as for me the nearness of God is my good; I have made the Lord God my refuge, that I may tell of all Thy works" (Psalm 73:25,28).

A SUMMARY

We obey God because. . .

1. Christ's love motivates us to live for Him.
2. Our Father lovingly disciplines us for wrongdoing.
3. Sin is destructive and should be avoided.
4. We will receive eternal rewards for obedience.
5. He is worthy of our obedience.

A BEGINNING EXERCISE

In order to help you experience God's truths, an exercise from the corresponding workbook is included at the conclusion of chapters 4, 5, 6, and 7 in the book.

How can we allow God to set us free from the fear of failure? How can we begin to live in light of justification? Applying what Christ said in the following verse of Scripture will help us get started:

"For in the way you judge, you will be judged; and by your standard of measure, it will be measured to you" (Matthew 7:2).

From this passage of Scripture and what we know about ourselves, we can draw the following conclusions and applications:

1. We use the same methods for judging others that we use to judge ourselves.

2. Though some of us are more reflective than others, all of us spend a great deal of time evaluating our performance.

3. At this point, we have a choice. We can use the same method we have always used to evaluate ourselves and others (Our Self-Worth = Performance + Others' Opinions), or we can adopt God's judgment (Our Self-Worth = God's Truth About Us).

4. If we want our lives to be what God has designed them to be, then we must use His truth as the standard of evaluation, rather than our own judgment.

5. To accomplish this change in mindset, we need to apply the following action points:

a. When we see another person, we should think, and if possible, state verbally, "This person has great worth apart from his performance because Christ gave His life for him, and therefore, imparted great value to him. If this person has accepted Christ, *he is deeply loved, fully pleasing, totally forgiven, accepted, and complete in Christ.*"

b. To those in our families who we know are Christians, we can tell them each day, "*You are deeply loved, fully pleasing, totally forgiven, accepted, and complete in Christ.*"

6. As you do this you will automatically begin to use the same system of evaluation on yourself, and thereby reinforce the truths in your own mind.

7. Failures, both in your own life and in the lives of your family, can be seen as opportunities to apply the Biblical value system. Affirmation of love and acceptance can be powerful in shaping a healthy self-concept!

God has given us the Bible as a guidebook. By understanding Biblical truths, we will be able to identify the deceptions of Satan; then we can reject these lies and replace them with the eternal truths from God's Word. This process is not easy, but it is essential to our sense of self-worth and our desire to honor Christ.

Chapter Five

Approval Addict

The perception of failure is at the root of a poor self-concept, but for many of us, the problem is not only how we view ourselves, it also includes how we think others perceive us. Basing our self-worth on what we believe others think about us causes us to be addicted to their approval.

Bob felt like a vending machine. Anyone wanting something from him could pull an invisible lever and get it. On the job, Bob was always doing other people's work for them. At home, his friends continually called on him to help in odd jobs around their houses. His wife had him working weekends just so she could continue in the lifestyle to which she had grown accustomed. Even people in Bob's church took advantage of him, knowing they could count on "good old Bob" to head up any program they planned. What was the problem? Was Bob simply a self-sacrificing saint? On the surface, yes; in reality, no. Bob deeply resented the people who demanded so much of him and left him with little time for himself. Yet, Bob just couldn't say "No." He longed for the approval of others and believed that agreeing to their every wish would win this approval for him.

Bob is typical of so many of us! We spend so much time building relationships, striving to please people and win their respect. But then, after all of our sincere, conscientious effort, it takes only one un-appreciative word from someone to ruin our sense of self-worth. How quickly an insensitive word can destroy the self-assurance we've worked so hard to achieve!

The world we live in is filled with people demanding that we please them in exchange for their approval and acceptance. Such demands lead us directly into a second false belief: *"I must be approved by certain others to feel good about myself."*

We are snared by this lie in many subtle ways. Our acceptance of this false belief causes us to bow to peer pressure in an effort to gain approval. We may join clubs and organizations hoping to find a place of acceptance for ourselves. We identify ourselves with social groups, believing that being with others like ourselves will assure our acceptance and their approval.

Many people have admitted that their experimentation with drugs or sex is a reaction to their need to belong. However, drugs and sexual promiscuity promised something they couldn't fulfill, and experimentation only left these people with pain and a deeper need for self-worth and acceptance.

To visualize the effects of Satan's lie: *"I must be approved by certain others to feel good about myself,"* consider the following analogy. In a person's brain, there are both pain and pleasure centers. Suppose someone implanted an electrode in each center. While a gifted professor eloquently expounds on the destructive effects of certain activities, someone else begins to send intense electrical impulses to the electrodes. When the person acts in a way that pleases the one at the electrode controls, an impulse is sent out to the pleasure center to indicate approval. When the person acts in a way that displeases the person at the controls, a sharp pain is the immediate result. Which one has more influence on the person, the eloquent professor or the one at the controls who gives immediate sensory feedback?

A similar scenario is played out daily in most of our lives. Our peer group corresponds to the person at the electrode controls, having the ability to give immediate approval or disapproval. No matter how well we have been taught by parents, pastors, or teachers, the influence of the peer group supersedes all else because it is profound and instantaneous. More teaching is not the answer. Motivating by fear or guilt is not ultimately productive. When the one at the controls of the electrodes is replaced, then the root cause of pain and pleasure will be changed. If we believe Satan's lies, we allow him to determine the basis of our self-worth. But if we reject his lies and value Christ's love and acceptance above all else, then we won't be dominated by the whims of our peers.

Another symptom of our fear of rejection is our inability to give and receive love. We find it difficult to open up and reveal our inner thoughts and motives because we believe that others will reject us if they know what we are really like. Therefore, our fear of rejection leads us to superficial relationships or isolation. Ironically, the more we experience isolation, the more we need acceptance. Eric Fromm once wrote, "The deep need of man is the need to overcome separateness, to leave the prison of his aloneness."

The fear of rejection is rampant, and loneliness is one of the most dangerous and widespread problems in America today. One recent study concluded that loneliness has already reached epidemic proportions in our country, and if it continues to spread, loneliness could seriously erode the emotional strength of our country. And loneliness is not relegated only to unbelievers. Ninety-two percent of the Christians attending a recent Bible conference admitted in a survey that feelings of loneliness were a major problem in their lives. All shared a basic symptom – a sense of despair at feeling unloved and a fear of being unwanted or unaccepted. That is a tragic commentary on the people about whom Christ said:

"By this all men will know that you are my disciples if you have love for one another" (John 13:35).

For the most part, our modern society has responded to rejection and loneliness in an inadequate way. Our response has been "outer-directed," meaning that we seek a stronger union with our fellow man by conforming to a group. We identify with the customs, dress, ideas, and patterns of behavior of a particular group, allowing the consensus of the group to determine what is correct for us. But conforming to a group does not provide the security we are so desperately seeking. Only God can provide that. The apostle Paul described the process of breaking free from the domination of the world's value system:

> *"Don't let the world around you squeeze you into its own mold, but let God remold your minds from within, so that you may prove in practice that the plan of God for you is good, meets all His demands, and moves toward the goal of true maturity" (Romans 12:2).*

Turning to others for what only God can provide is a direct result of our acceptance of Satan's lie:

Self-Worth = Performance + Others' Opinions

Living according to the false belief: *"I must be approved by certain others to feel good about myself,"* causes us to continually fear rejection, conforming virtually all of our attitudes and actions to the expectations of others. How are you affected by this belief? Take the test on the following page to determine how strongly you fear rejection.

FEAR OF REJECTION TEST

Read each statement. Look at the top of the test and choose the term which best describes your response. Put the number above that term in the blank beside the statement.

1	2	3	4	5	6	7
Always	Very Often	Often	Sometimes	Seldom	Very Seldom	Never

_____1. I avoid certain people.

_____2. When I sense I might be rejected by someone, I become nervous and anxious.

____3.   I am uncomfortable around those who are different from me.

____4.   It bothers me when someone is unfriendly to me.

____5.   I am basically shy and unsocial.

____6.   I am critical of others.

____7.   I find myself trying to impress others.

____8.   I become depressed when someone criticizes me.

____9.   I always try to determine what people think of me.

____10.   I don't understand people and what motivates them.

____ Total (Add up the numbers you have placed in the blanks.)

INTERPRETATION OF SCORE

If your score is...

57-70

God apparently has released you from the fear of rejection that plagues most people. The major exceptions to this are those who are greatly deceived or have become callous to their own emotions as a way to suppress the pain.

47-56

The fear of rejection rarely or only in certain situations controls your experiences. Again, the only major exception involves those who are not honest with themselves.

37-46

When you experience emotional problems, they may relate to a sense of rejection. In looking back, you can probably relate many of your decisions to this fear. Many of your decisions in the future will also be affected by the fear of rejection unless you take direct action to overcome it.

27-36

Not only is the above category true of your experiences, but this fear of rejection forms a general backdrop to your life. There are probably few days that you are not affected in some way by the fear of rejection. Unfortunately, this also robs you of the joy and peace your salvation was meant to bring.

0-26

Experiences of rejection dominate your memory and have probably resulted in a great deal of depression. These problems will persist until some definitive action is taken. In other words, this condition will not simply disappear; time alone cannot heal your pain. You must deal with the root issue.

THE EFFECTS OF THE FEAR OF REJECTION

Virtually all of us fear rejection. We can fall prey to it even when we try to harden our defenses in anticipation of someone's disapproval. Defense mechanisms of withdrawal or being sure to please others' every whim are not the answer. They may dull the pain temporarily, but they don't deal with the real problem.

In its basic form, rejection is a type of communication. It communicates to another individual how little we respect him. Rejection may come in the form of an outburst of anger, a disgusted look, an impatient answer, or a social snub. Whatever the form, rejection carries a universal message of disrespect, low value, and lack of appreciation. Nothing hurts like the message of rejection.

If this is true, why do we use rejection so frequently? One reason is that rejection is a very effective, though destructive, motivator. Think about it: Without laying a hand on anyone, we can send the message that our targeted individual doesn't measure up. We can harness that individual's instinctive desire for acceptance until we have changed and adapted his behavior to suit our tastes and purposes. Therefore, rejection enables us to control the actions of another human being.

Many misguided preachers have used rejection and guilt as a forceful means of motivation. They expound upon our weaknesses, our failures, and unworthiness, and our inability to measure up to Christ's high standards. Not only is our performance declared unworthy, but we are left feeling denounced, devalued, and devastated. As a result, thousands who have been broken by this rejection have left the church without understanding Christ's accepting, unconditional love, a love that never uses condemnation to correct behavior.

However, rejection and guilt are only effective as long as we can keep people near us. This is why certain parental techniques of guilt motivation are effective only until the child matures and gains more freedom. With the freedom, the child is able to remove himself physically from his parents. Then he is unrestrained and can do whatever he pleases. Many parents are confused by what happens, but most of them could trace their child's "sudden rebellion" to the guilt they have communicated to their children over the years.

Although rejection can control others, it can also isolate them. For example, Randy was raised in a broken home, living with his father since he was six. It wasn't that Randy's father wanted him, but his mother was too busy to care for him. Shortly after the divorce, Randy's father married another woman with three children. Eventually, Randy's stepmother began to resent any time or effort she spent on him. She favored her own children at Randy's expense.

It is no surprise, then, that when Randy grew up and married a beautiful girl who truly loved him, he was cautious about giving his love. Randy had experienced the pain of rejection all of his life and now, because he feared rejection, he withdrew his love from someone he truly cared for. Randy was afraid to become too close because if his wife rejected him, the pain would be too much for him to bear.

How do you react to the fear of rejection? Some of us project a cool, impervious exterior, never developing deep, satisfying relationships. Some of us are so fearful of rejection that we withdraw and say "no" to anyone and any request, while others continually say "yes" so people will be pleased with them. Some are shy and easily manipulated, while others are sensitive to criticism and react defensively. A deep fear of failure may even cause some to be hostile and others to develop nervous disorders.

Our fear of rejection exists only because we base our self-worth on the opinions of others rather than our relationship with God. Our dependence on others for value brings bondage, while abiding in the truths of Christ's love and acceptance brings freedom and joy.

In Galatians 1:10, Paul clearly draws the line concerning our search for approval:

> *"For am I now seeking the favor of men, or of God? Or am I striving to please men? If I were still trying to please men, I would not be a bondservant of Christ."*

According to this passage, we can ultimately seek either the approval of men or the approval of God as the basis of our self-worth. We cannot seek both. God wants to be the Lord of our lives, and He is unwilling to share that rightful Lordship with anyone else.

Therefore, the only way we can overcome rejection is to value the constant approval of God over the conditional approval of people. God's love and acceptance is the source of great freedom, joy, and positive motivation. According to Luke 4:18, Christ was sent *"to proclaim release to the captives, and recovery of sight to the blind, to set free those who are downtrodden. . . ."*

Similar to the fear of failure, the fear of rejection can affect our lives in many ways. The explanations of the following symptoms are not exhaustive, but are intended to demonstrate how rejection can trigger certain problems in our lives.

Anger, Resentment, Hostility

Anger is the most common response to rejection. If this anger is not adequately dealt with, it can result in deep resentment and hostility. However, these two emotions are generally reserved for those whose fear of failure has permanently scarred them. The primary motive for retaining anger is the desire for revenge.

Being Easily Manipulated

People who believe that their self-worth is based on the approval of others will do virtually anything to please other people. These people truly believe they will be well liked if they agree to every request of those manipulating them. However, in reality, many of these people often despise those manipulating them and resent what they have to do to earn their approval.

Avoiding People

Among the most common ways people react to their fear of rejection is to avoid people, thereby avoiding the risk of rejection. Some people avoid others overtly, spending most of their time alone, but most people try to lower the risk of rejection by having superficial relationships. They may be around people much of the time, and they may be considered socially adept because they know how to make friends easily, but these "friends" never really get to know them because they hide behind a wall of words, smiles, and activities. These people are quite lonely in the midst of all their "friends."

Domineering

In an effort to avoid being hurt by others, many people are constantly trying to maintain control of people and dominate every situation. They have become experts in controlling others by dispensing approval or disapproval. They are unwilling to let others be themselves and make their own decisions without giving their consent or disapproval. Because such people are actually very insecure, lack of control is an unacceptable threat to them.

Schizophrenia

Schizophrenia is a disorder in which people fashion their own make-believe worlds. Those suffering from schizophrenia attempt to escape social interaction. Unwilling to accept the pain of disapproval, these people see escape as their last, or only, option.

Depression

Depression is the result of repressed, pent-up anger. When anger is not handled properly, the body and mind respond to the intense pressure, and the person's emotions and sense of purpose become dulled. Depression, then, is the body's way of deadening the destructive effects of repressed anger.

The reason we experience the problems that accompany the fear of rejection is because we believe Satan's lie that our **Self-Worth = Performance + Others' Opinions**. We crave love, fellowship, and intimacy, and we turn to others to meet those needs. However, the problem with basing our worth on the approval of others is that people often fail to love and appreciate us unconditionally. But there is another way. God has provided a solution to the experience and fear of rejection.

GOD'S ANSWER: RECONCILIATION

God's solution to the fear of rejection is based on Christ's sacrificial payment for our sins. Through this payment, we find forgiveness, reconciliation, and total acceptance through Christ. Reconciliation means that those who were enemies have become friends. Paul described our transformation from enmity to friendship with God:

> *"Although you were formerly alienated and hostile in your mind, engaged in evil deeds, yet He has now reconciled you in His fleshly body through death, in order to present you before Him holy and blameless and beyond reproach"* *(Colossians 1:21,22).*

As I talked with Pam, it became obvious that she did not understand this great truth of reconciliation. Three years into her marriage, Pam had committed adultery with a man at her office. The guilt that plagued her made it hard for her to feel acceptable to God. Her guilt persisted even though she had confessed her sin to God and to her husband, and both had forgiven her. Four years after the affair, she still could not forgive herself for what she had done.

Finally as we talked, I became frustrated with her reluctance to believe that she was forgiven by God. I told her, "But to hear you tell it, one would think God could never forgive you of a sin like that."

"That's right," she replied. "I don't think He ever will."

"But God doesn't base His love and acceptance of us on our performance," I stated. "If ever there is a sin so filthy and vile that makes us less acceptable to Him, then the cross is insufficient. If the cross isn't sufficient for any particular sin, then the Bible is in error when it says that he forgave all your sins"(Colossians 2:13-15). God took our sins and cancelled them by nailing them to Christ's cross. In this way God also took away Satan's power to condemn us for sin. So you see, nothing you will ever do can nullify your reconciliation and make you unacceptable to God.

All of us need to realize the truth I was trying to communicate to Pam. Salvation is not simply a ticket to heaven. It is the beginning of a dynamic new relationship with God. Justification is the doctrine that explains the judicial facts of our forgiveness and righteousness in Christ. Reconciliation explains the relational aspect of our salvation. The moment we receive Christ by faith, we enter into a personal relationship with Him. We are united with God in an eternal and inseparable bond (Romans 8:38,39). We are bound in an indissoluble union with him, as a joint-heir with Christ. The Holy Spirit has sealed us in that relationship, and we are absolutely secure in Christ. Ephesians 1:13, 14 states:

> "Having also believed, you were sealed in Him with the Holy Spirit of promise, Who is given as a pledge of our inheritance, with a view to the redemption of God's own possession, to the praise of His glory."

Recently, in a group prayer meeting someone prayed, "Thank you, God, for accepting me when I am so unacceptable." That person understood that we cannot become acceptable through our own merit, but he seems to have forgotten that we are unconditionally accepted in Christ. We are no longer unacceptable. That is the point of the cross. Through Christ's death and resurrection, we have become acceptable to God. That did not occur because God decided He could overlook our sin. It occurred because Christ forgave all our sins so that He could present us to the Father, holy and blameless.

There is no greater theme in Scripture than the reconciliation of man to God. Open your Bible and read for yourself. Study the following passages of Scripture, and then answer the questions after each one:

1. EPHESIANS 2:8,9 - On what basis could we boast?
2. GALATIANS 2:16 - On what basis are we justified?
3. ACTS 10:43 - Of what did the prophets bear witness?
4. ROMANS 5:10 - Through what are we reconciled?
5. GALATIANS 3:6 - On what basis did Abraham receive righteousness?
6. II CORINTHIANS 5:17,19,21 - Describe what we are in Christ.
7. GALATIANS 2:16 - What part do works play in justification?
8. ROMANS 4:7 - Who is blessed?
9. HEBREWS 9:22 - What would you have to do in order to receive forgiveness?
10. JOHN 5:24 - What is the promise to the person who knows and believes?
11. EPHESIANS 1:7 - According to what do we receive forgiveness?
12. PSALM 103:12 - What happens to our transgressions?
13. HEBREWS 10:18 - After forgiveness, what is to be our offering for sin?
14. HEBREWS 12:2 - Who is the perfecter of our faith?
15. JOHN 3:16 - What is God's promise?
16. MATTHEW 26:28 - Why was Christ's blood shed?
17. ACTS 13:39 - What does belief do?
18. ROMANS 3:23,24 - By what are we justified?
19. JOHN 10:27-29 - What do His sheep have? Will they perish?
20. ROMANS 8:28-39 - Of what is Paul convinced?
21. I PETER 1:3,4 - Of what is Peter convinced?
22. ROMANS 8:33 - Who shall accuse us?

23.   ROMANS 8:15-17 - Describe the nature of our relationship with God.

Because of reconciliation, we are completely acceptable to God and accepted by God. As these passages illustrate, we enjoy a full and complete relationship with God, and in this relationship, our value is not based on our performance.

However, we may question what this relationship means as we attempt to apply it in our day-to-day experience. Dozens of people have voiced this same question to me. Let's analyze this issue: When we are born again as spiritual beings in right standing with God, we are not yet fully mature. As new spiritual people, we find ourselves still tilted towards the world's way of thinking. Because we have been conditioned by the world's perspective and values, we find it hard to break away. Indeed, when Paul wrote the Christians at Corinth, he called them "men of flesh" and "babes in Christ." Though born of the Spirit and equipped with all provisions in Christ, these individuals had yet to develop into the complete, mature believers God intended them to be (I Corinthians 3:3,4).

Many of us are like the Christians at Corinth. As young and inexperienced babes in Christ, we still try to get our significance the world's way: through success and approval. Often, we look only to other believers rather than to Christ Himself. We learn to use the right Christian words, claim divine power and guidance, and organize programs, and yet so often, our spiritual facade lacks depth and substance. Our spiritual activities become human efforts lacking the real touch of the Master.

The Christian who still depends on his success and seeks the approval of others for his self-worth is a Christian who has barely begun on his spiritual journey toward maturity. Success and approval constitute the basis of an addictive, worldly, carnal self-worth. Certainly, withdrawal from this view may cause us some pain as we change the basis of our self-worth, yet we will discover true freedom and maturity in Christ only when we understand that our lives mean much more than success or the approval of others.

Moreover, the person who will not value God's opinion over his abilities to please others is a prideful individual. Make no mistake about it, we can do nothing to contribute to Christ's free gift of salvation: furthermore, if we base our self-worth on the approval of others, then we are actually saying that our ability to please others is of greater worth than Christ's payment. We are the sinners, the depraved, the wretched, and the helpless. He is the loving Father, the seeking, searching, patient Savior who has made atonement for the lost and extended grace and sonship. We add nothing to our salvation. It is God who seeks us out, convicts us of sin, and reveals Himself to us; it is God who gives us the very faith with which to accept Him! Our faith is simply our response to what He has done for us.

The Christian who embraces the measureless gift of God to man gladly surrenders his pride. Realizing God's love, forgiveness, and acceptance enables us to end our struggle for success and approval. All the time, energy, and effort we have spent to achieve respect and success cannot compare to the contentment and joy found in the unconditional acceptance of Christ.

So then, our worth lies in the fact that Christ's blood has paid for our sins, therefore, we are reconciled to God. We are accepted on that basis alone, but does this great truth indicate that we don't need other people in our lives? On the contrary, God very often uses other believers to demonstrate His love and His acceptance to us. The strength, comfort, encouragement, and love of Christians toward one another is a visible expression of the love of God. However, our acceptance and worth are not dependent on others' acceptance of us, even if they are fellow-believers! Whether they accept us or not, we are still deeply loved, completely forgiven, fully pleasing, totally accepted, and complete in Christ. He alone is the final authority on our worth and acceptance.

A BEGINNING EXERCISE

How do we learn to reject Satan's lie, *"I must be approved by certain others to feel good about myself"*? How can we begin to practically apply the great truth of our reconciliation to Almighty God? The following exercise will help you begin to experience the freedom and joy of reconciliation. Consider this passage from Revelation:

> "*And I heard a loud voice in heaven, saying, 'Now the salvation, and the power, and the kingdom of our God and the authority of His Christ have come, for the accuser of our brethren has been thrown down, who accuses them before our God day and night. And they overcame him because of the blood of the Lamb and because of the word of their testimony, and they did not love their life even to death*" (*Revelation 12: 10,11*).

How are we going to overcome Satan, the accuser, and experience our acceptance in Christ? According to this passage of Scripture, there is only one way, by the blood of the Lamb. First of all, we must stop trying to overcome our feelings of condemnation and failure by penitent actions. Defending ourselves or trying to pay for our sins by our actions leads only to a guilt and penance spiral because we can never do enough on our own. No matter how much we do to make up for the sin, we still feel guilty and we feel like we need to do more. We can only resist Satan, the accuser of the brethren, because Christ's blood has completely paid for our sins and delivered us from guilt.

Secondly, we need to verbalize what the blood of Christ has done for us: *We are deeply loved, completely forgiven, fully pleasing, totally accepted, and complete in Christ.*

As the Bible says in Revelation 12:11, we should not love our lives (dictated by what seems reasonable to us) to the point of spiritual deadness. Love for the world and its pleasures renders us spiritually impotent. We must decide that our minds are no longer the source of truth and instead, get our knowledge, wisdom, and direction from the Scriptures. There are two practical steps that will help make these truths a reality in our lives:

1.　　On one side of a 3 x 5 card, write the following:

Because of Christ and His redemption,
I am completely forgiven and fully pleasing to God.
I am totally accepted by God.

2.   On the other side of the card write out Romans 5:1 and Colossians 1:21,22.

Carry this card with you for the next 28 days. Every time you get something to drink, look at the card and remind yourself of what Christ has done for you. If you do this consistently for 28 days, these truths will come to your mind for the rest of your life. As you read and memorize these statements and passages, think about how they apply to you. Memorization and application of these truths will have profound effects as your mind is transformed by God's Word.

Chapter Six

The Blame Game

Our perception of success and failure is our primary basis of evaluating people. If we believe that failure (either our own or others') makes a person unacceptable and unworthy of love, then we will feel completely justified in condemning that person. This condemnation can be harsh (physical or verbal abuse), or it can be relatively subtle (sarcasm or silence). But any form of condemnation is a powerfully destructive force which communicates, "I'll make you sorry for what you did."

Matt made a serious mistake early in his life and was never able to overcome it. At fourteen, he and several friends from school stepped inside a downtown department store and tried to slip out with half a dozen record albums without paying for them. They made it to the glass doors past the cashier's stand before a security guard caught them and escorted all of them into the manager's office.

Matt never heard the end of the incident. From then on, every time he made a mistake at home, his father reminded him what had happened. "You're a colossal failure!" his father would scream.

"You've got no values whatsoever! You're a liar and a thief, and you'll never amount to anything!"

Matt was never able to forget his humiliation. At age twenty, he sat in my office and told me very seriously that some days he was happy until he recognized he was feeling good. Believing that he had no right to feel good about himself, he would begin to feel depressed again.

"After all," he reflected, "no one as worthless as I am should feel good about himself."

Like so many others, Matt had been brainwashed and broken by the third false belief: *"Those who fail are unworthy of love and deserve to be punished."*

Whether consciously or unconsciously, we all tend to point an accusing finger, assigning blame for virtually every failure. Whenever we fail to receive approval for our performance, we search for a reason, a culprit, a scapegoat. More likely than not, we can find no one but ourselves to blame so the accusing finger points right back at us. Self-condemnation is often a severe form of punishment.

If possible, we will try to place the blame on others and fulfill the law of retribution – that people should get what they deserve. All our lives we have been conditioned to make someone pay for every failure or shortcoming. When a deadline is missed at work, we let everyone know it's not our fault: "I know the report was due yesterday, but Frank didn't get me the statistics until this morning." If a household chore is left undone, we instantly look to the other family members to determine who is responsible. For every flaw we see around us, we search for someone to blame, hoping to exonerate ourselves by making sure the one who failed is properly identified and punished.

Another reason we seek to blame others is that our success often depends on the contribution of others and their failure is a threat to us. Because their failure blocks our goal of success, we respond by defending ourselves and blaming them. Blaming them helps put a safe distance between their failure and our fragile self-worth.

This pattern is evident in the case of Ellen. When Ellen discovered that her fifteen-year-old daughter was pregnant, she went a week without sleep, tossing and turning, trying to discover who was to blame. Was it only her daughter who had brought this reproach on the family, or was she to blame for failing as a mother? All Ellen knew was that someone had to take responsibility.

Rather than working out our problems rationally by evaluating our performance and improving on it, we either accuse someone else or berate ourselves. These reactions produce either a critical attitude or self-condemnation, both of which result in an erosion of self-confidence.

Yet another reason we blame others is to make ourselves feel better. By blaming someone else who failed, we feel superior. In fact, the higher the position of the one who failed (parent, boss, pastor, etc.), the farther they fall and the better we feel. This desire to be superior, to be "one up on them," is at the root of gossip.

How should we respond when people fail? If the person who failed is a Christian, we need to affirm God's truth about him: *He is deeply loved by God, completely forgiven, fully pleasing, totally accepted by God, and complete in Christ.* This perspective can change our attitude from condemnation to love and a desire to help. By believing these truths, we will be able to love the person just as God loves us (I John 4:11), forgive him just as God has forgiven us (Ephesians 4:32), and accept him just as God has accepted us (Romans 15:7). This does not mean that we will become blind to others' faults or failures. We will still see them, but our response to them will change considerably, from condemnation to compassion. As our self-worth is less dependent on other people, their sins and mistakes will become less of a threat to us, and we will want to help them instead of punish them.

But what about our response to unbelievers? Although they haven't yet trusted in the cross of Christ to have their condemnation taken away, Jesus was very clear about how we should treat them. In

Matthew 22: 36-39, He told His disciples to love the Lord your God, with all your heart, soul, and mind, and also, to *"love your neighbor* (both believers and unbelievers) *as yourself."* Jesus was even more specific in Luke 6:27,28. He said, *"But I say to you who hear, love your enemies, do good to those who hate you, bless those who curse you, pray for those who mistreat you."* Christ didn't come to love and die for the lovely, righteous people of the world. If He had, we would all be in trouble! Instead, He came to love and die for the unrighteous, the inconsiderate, and the selfish. As we understand His love for us, and that He rescued us from the righteous condemnation we deserve because of our sins, we will be more patient and kind to others when they fail. It can be very helpful if we compare the failure or sin of others with our sins that Christ died to forgive: *"There is nothing that anyone can do to me that can compare with my sin of rebellion that Christ has completely forgiven."* That should give us a lot of perspective!

We tend to make two major errors when we punish others for their failures. The first error is that we condemn people not only for genuine sin, but also for their mistakes. When people have tried their best and failed, they do not need our biting blame. They need our love and encouragement. We also tend to blame others because their actions (whether the actions were overt disobedience or honest mistakes) make us look like failures, and our own failure is unacceptable to us. Relationships like husband - wife, parent - child, and employer - employee, are especially vulnerable to one person being threatened by the failure of another: a wife gets angry at her husband for his not-so-funny joke at an important dinner party; a parent erupts at a child for accidentally spilling milk; or a manager scowls at an employee because an error in the employee's calculations has made him look foolish to his supervisor. People generally have a difficult time dealing with their sins; let's not compound their problems by condemning them for their mistakes.

A second major error we often make when we condemn others is that we believe that we are the agents of condemnation. We seem to possess a great need to balance the scales of right and wrong, and we cannot tolerate injustice. We are correct in recognizing that sin is reprehensible and deserves condemnation, yet we have not been licensed by God to punish sin. Judgment is God's responsibility, not man's. Jesus dealt specifically with this issue when several men decided to stone a woman caught in adultery. He told them that the person without sin should throw the first stone. Beginning with the eldest, all of the accusers walked away as they remembered their own sinfulness. In light of their own sinfulness, they no longer saw fit to condemn the sins of another. As this incident clearly points out, we should leave righteous condemnation and punishment in the hands of the One worthy of the responsibility. Our response should be love, affirmation, and possibly, compassionate correction.

When someone acts in a way that is offensive or insulting to us, should we tell them that they have made us angry or hurt our feelings? Many psychologists say that venting our emotions is the right response because repression is unhealthy, but this advice misses two important points: *why* do we tell the person we are upset, and *who* is the most appropriate person to tell? In his book The Marriage Builder, Larry Crabb explains that the reason for any and all communication with another person should be to minister to him and help him, not just to vent our emotions. If we realize that our needs for security and purpose are fully met in Christ, and an insult is not a threat to our self-worth, then our goal in relationships is no longer to make us feel better about ourselves. Our security is no longer threatened by others, so we can give our attention to helping them instead of being preoccupied with how they have hurt or offended us. Consequently, we can love and accept others even when they are rude and insulting – just as Christ loves and accepts us. Expressing our feelings so people will treat us in the way we want to be treated is a form of manipulation, not love.

Accepting and loving people just as Christ accepts and loves us does not mean that our emotions toward the one who has been inconsiderate will always be warm and tender. Love and acceptance of others are often in spite of very real feelings of hurt or anger. And this hurt or anger should not be repressed. It should be expressed fully to the appropriate person – the Lord. The point is this: we should express our painful emotions fully to the Lord, and then communicate whatever will be most helpful to the one who has offended us. In this way, we neither repress our emotions nor respond to others in a reactionary, manipulative way.

We have a choice in our response to failure: We can condemn or we can learn. All of us fail, but this doesn't mean that we are failures. We need to understand that failing can be a step toward maturity, not a permanent blot on our self-esteem. Like children, we all stumble and fall. And, just like children first learning to walk, we can pick ourselves up and begin again. We don't have to allow failure to prevent us from being used by God.

God forgives His children and wants us to experience His forgiveness on a daily basis. For example, Moses was a murderer, but God forgave him and used him to deliver Israel from Egypt. David was an adulterer and a murderer, but God forgave him and made him a great king. Peter denied the Lord, but God forgave him and Peter became a leader in the church. God rejoices when His children learn to accept His forgiveness, pick themselves up, and walk after they have stumbled. But, in addition, we must learn to forgive ourselves. We need to take our sins and failures to Christ and rejoice in His forgiveness.

Many psychologists today adhere to a theory called Rational Emotive Therapy. This very helpful theory states that blame is the core of most emotional disturbances. The answer, they insist, is for each of us to stop blaming ourselves and others, and learn to accept ourselves in spite of imperfection. How right they are! Christ's death is the complete payment for sin, and we can claim His complete forgiveness and acceptance.

Thousands of emotional problems are rooted in the false belief that we must meet certain standards to be acceptable, and that the only way to deal with inadequacies is to punish ourselves and others for them. There is no way we can shoulder such a heavy burden. Our guilt will overpower us and the weight of our failures will break us.

This third false belief: *"Those who fail (including myself) are unworthy of love and deserve to be punished,"* is the root of our fear of punishment and our desire to punish others. How deeply are you affected by this lie? Take the test on the following page to determine how great an influence it has in your life.

FEAR OF PUNISHMENT/PUNISHING OTHERS TEST

Read each statement. Look at the top of the test and choose the term which best describes your response. Put the number above that term in the blank beside the statement.

1	2	3	4	5	6	7
Always	Very Often	Often	Sometimes	Seldom	Very Seldom	Never

_____1.   I fear what God might do to me.

_____2.   After I fail, I worry about God's response.

_____3.   When I see someone in a difficult situation, I wonder what they did to deserve their problems.

_____4.   When something goes wrong, I have a tendency to think God must be punishing me.

_____5.   I am very hard on myself when I fail.

_____6.   I find myself wanting to blame people when they fail.

_____7.   I get angry at God when someone immoral or dishonest prospers.

____8.   I am compelled to tell others when I see them doing wrong.

____9.   I tend to focus on the faults and failures of others.

____10.   God seems harsh to me.

____ Total (Add up the numbers you have placed in the blanks.)

INTERPRETATION OF SCORE

If your score is...

57-70

God apparently has released you from the fear of punishment that plagues most people. The major exceptions to this are those who are either greatly deceived or have become callous to their own emotions as a way to suppress the pain.

47-56

The fear of punishment and the desire to punish others rarely or only in certain situations control your experience. Again, the only major exception involves those who are not honest with themselves.

37-46

When you experience emotional problems, they may tend to relate to a fear of punishment or a desire to punish others. In looking back, you can probably relate many of your decisions to this fear. Many of your decisions in the future will also be affected by the fear of punishment or the desire to punish others unless you take direct action to overcome this tendency.

27-36

Not only is the above category true of your experience, but this fear of punishment forms a general backdrop to your life. There are probably few days that you are not affected in some way by the fear of punishment and the propensity to blame others. Unfortunately, this also robs you of the joy and peace your salvation was meant to bring.

0-26

Experiences of punishment dominate your memory, and you probably have experienced a great deal of depression. These problems will remain until some definitive plan is followed. In other words, this condition will not simply disappear; time alone cannot heal your pain. You must deal with the root issue.

THE EFFECTS OF THE FEAR OF PUNISHMENT AND THE DESIRE TO PUNISH OTHERS

Fear can take a deadly toll on people. Although the death certificate lists another disease, many times the true cause of death was the stress created by so many fears. The logical result of Satan's deception, Self-worth = Performance + Others' Opinions, is fear – fear of failure, rejection, and punishment. Many of us are so motivated by fear that we can't imagine what our lives would be like without it. and we have determined that failure must be punished. So as a result, we victimize ourselves and others by punishing virtually every failure we see.

We are the first and most obvious victims in this pattern of punishment. After failing, we may believe we must feel remorse for a certain length of time before we can experience peace and joy again. In a twisted form of self-motivation, we believe that if we condemn ourselves enough, then perhaps we won't fail again.

Not only do we victimize ourselves by this thinking, but we also practice judgment on others. Ironically, the people we judge the harshest are those we love and need the most. This reaction is a response to our great need for consistency and justice. If we are going to punish failure in ourselves, we reason that we must be consistent and punish failure in others. Also, insisting on justice, we take it upon ourselves to be God's instrument of correction. We don't like to see others getting away with something that should be punished (or perhaps that we wish we could do ourselves!).

In a sense, the final victim in such a situation is God. Although God is not truly a victim, actions such as these distort our perception of Him. This distortion of our perception of God can have two effects. First, many people are convinced that every painful circumstance in their lives is punishment from God. These people see themselves as more compassionate than God, knowing they would never treat their children the way their Heavenly Father treats them.

A second reaction is to completely turn from God and His principles. Rationalizing that punishment is inevitable, some people decide to "live it up" and enjoy their sin before the judgment comes.

The fear of punishment and punishing others can affect our lives in many ways. Here is a brief description of some of the most common problems:

Self-induced Punishment

Many of us operate on the theory that if we are hard enough on ourselves, then God won't have to punish us. However, we fail to realize that God disciplines us in love but never punishes us in anger. If God does not punish us, we don't need to punish ourselves.

Bitterness

If we believe that God and others are always punishing us, soon we will become quite angry. Harboring this anger and always questioning God's motives will result in deep bitterness and pessimism.

Passivity

Fear of punishment is at the root of one of the most common problems in our society: passivity. Passivity is the neglect of our minds, time, gifts, or talents, through inaction. God intends for us to actively cooperate with Him, but fear immobilizes our wills. Passivity results in a dull life, avoiding risks and missing opportunities.

Punishing Others

Our specific response to the failure of others depends on several factors: our personalities, the nature of their failure, and how their failure reflects on us (i.e., if their failure makes us look like we failed: "His mistake makes me look like I'm dumb," or ". . . a bad parent," or ". . . a poor leader," or ". . . a rotten employee," etc.). Our condemnation of those who fail may take the form of verbal abuse, physical abuse, nagging criticism, withholding appreciation and affection, or ignoring them. All of these responses are designed to "make them pay for what they did."

The fear of punishment and the desire to punish others can be overcome by realizing that Christ bore the punishment we deserved. His motives toward us are loving and kind. His discipline is designed to correct us and to protect us from the destruction of sin, not to punish us.

GOD'S ANSWER: PROPITIATION

When Christ died on the cross, He was our substitute. He took the righteous wrath of God that we deserved. The depth of God's love for us is revealed by the extremity of His actions for us: the holy Son of God became a man and died a horrible death in our place. Two passages state this eloquently. Isaiah anticipated the Christ who would come:

> *"Surely our griefs He Himself bore, and our sorrows He carried; yet we ourselves esteemed Him stricken smitten, of God, and afflicted. But He was pierced through for our transgressions, He was crushed for our iniquities; the chastening for our well-being fell upon Him, and by His scourging we are healed. All of us like sheep have gone astray, each of us*

has turned to his own way; but the Lord has caused the iniq-
uity of us all to fall on Him" (Isaiah 53:4-6).

And from the New Testament:

"By this the love of God was manifested in us, that God
has sent His only begotten Son into the world so that we
might live through Him. In this is love, not that we loved
God, but that He loved us and sent His Son to be the
propitiation for our sins. Beloved, if God so loved us, we
also ought to love one another" (I John 4:9-11).

Propitiation means to satisfy the wrath of someone who has
been unjustly wronged. Propitiation is an act that soothes hostility and
satisfies the need for vengeance. Providing His only begotten Son as
the propitiation for our sins was the greatest possible demonstration
of God's love for man.

To understand God's wondrous provision of propitiation, it is
helpful to remember what He has endured from mankind. From
Adam and Eve's sin in the Garden of Eden to the obvious depravity
we see in our world today, human history is mainly the story of greed,
hatred, lust, and pride – evidences of man's wanton rebellion against
the God of love and peace. If not done from a desire to glorify God,
even the "good" things people do are like filthy garments to God
(Isaiah 64:6).

Our sin deserves the righteous wrath of God. He is the Almighty, the rightful judge of the universe. He is absolutely holy and
perfect. *"God is light, and in Him there is no darkness at all" (1 John*
1:5). Because of these attributes, God cannot overlook sin, nor can He
compromise and accept sin. For God to condone even one sin would
defile His holiness like smearing a white satin wedding gown with
black tar. Also, because He is holy, God reacts in righteous anger in
His aversion to sin.

However, God is not only righteously indignant about sin, He also is a God of infinite love. In His holiness, God condemns sin, but in the most awesome example of love the world has ever seen, He ordained that His Son would die to pay for our sins. God sacrificed the sinless, perfect Savior to turn away, to propitiate, His great wrath.

And for whom did Christ die? Was it for the saints who honored Him? Was it for a world that appreciated His sinless life and worshipped Him? No! Christ died for us, while we were yet in our rebellion against Him:

> *"For while we were still helpless, at the right time Christ died for the ungodly. For one will hardly die for a righteous man; though perhaps for the good man someone would dare even to die. But God demonstrates His own love toward us, in that while we were yet sinners, Christ died for us. Much more then, having now been justified by His blood, we shall be saved from the wrath of God through Him. For if while we were enemies, we were reconciled to God through the death of His Son, much more, having been reconciled, we shall be saved by His life. And not only this, but we also exult in God through our Lord Jesus Christ, through whom we have now received the reconciliation" (Romans 5:6-11).*

Who can measure the fathomless depth of love that sent Christ to the cross? While we were the enemies of God, Christ averted the wrath we deserved so that we might become the sons of God. Dallas Holm, an outstanding contemporary Christian composer and musician, wrote a beautiful song of this majestic, unselfish deed, seen through the eyes of a father:

> *"Now I am a man, and have a baby of my own,*
> *I wonder, could I send my baby off all alone,*
> *To help someone, somewhere, somehow,*
> *To set some captive free.*

I wonder, could I do the same as what He did for me?"

What can we say of our holy Heavenly Father? Surely He did not escape seeing Christ's mistreatment at the hands of sinful men – the scourgings, the humiliation, the beatings. Surely He who spoke the world into being could have delivered Christ from the entire ordeal. And yet, the God of heaven peered down through time and saw you and me. Though we were His enemies, He loved us and longed to rescue us from our sins, and the sinless Christ became our substitute. Only Christ could avert God's righteous wrath against sin, so in love, the Father kept silent as Jesus hung from the cross. All His anger, all the wrath we would ever deserve, was piled upon Christ, and Christ became sin for us (II Corinthians 5:21). He bore His Father's anger and became the propitiation for our sins! He paid the penalty for our sins, and God's wrath was avenged. No longer does He look upon us through the eyes of judgment, but now He lavishes His love upon us. The Scriptures teach that absolutely nothing can separate us from His love (Romans 8:38, 39). He has adopted us (Romans 8:15) into a tender, intimate, and powerful relationship with Him.

Because we are His children, performance is no longer the basis of our worth. We are unconditionally and deeply loved by God, and we can live by faith in His grace. We were spiritually dead, but He has made us alive and given us the high status of sonship to the Almighty God. It will take all of eternity to comprehend the wealth of His love and grace. Paul explains this incomprehensible gift this way:

"But God, being rich in mercy, because of His great love with which He loved us, even when we were dead in our transgressions, made us alive together with Christ (by grace you have been saved), and raised us up with Him, and seated us with Him in the heavenly places, in Christ Jesus, in order that in the ages to come He might show the surpassing riches of His grace in kindness toward us in Christ Jesus. For by grace you have been saved through faith; and that not of

*yourselves, it is the gift of God; not as a result of works, that
no one should boast" (Ephesians 2:4-9).*

Propitiation, then, means that Christ has satisfied the holy wrath
of God through His payment for sin. There was only one reason for
Him to do it: He loves us. Infinitely, eternally, unconditionally, ir-
revocably, He loves us. God the Father loves us with the love of a
father, reaching to snatch us from harm. God the Son loves us with
the love of a brother, laying down His life for us. He alone has turned
away God's wrath from us. There is nothing we can do, no amount of
good deeds we can accomplish and no religious ceremonies we can
perform that can pay for our sins. But Christ conclusively paid for
them so that we can escape eternal condemnation and experience His
love and purposes both now and forever.

Christ not only paid for our sins at a point in time, He continues
to love us and teach us day after day. We have a weapon to use
against Satan as he attacks us with doubts about God's love for us.
Our weapon is the fact that Christ took our punishment upon Himself
at Calvary. We no longer have to fear punishment for our sins because
Christ paid for them all – past, present, and future. This tremendous
truth of propitiation clearly demonstrates that we are truly and deeply
loved by God. His perfect love casts out all fear as we allow it to flood
our hearts (I John 4:18).

A BEGINNING EXERCISE

How do we free ourselves from Satan's lie: *"Those who fail are
unworthy of love and deserve to be punished"?* We are freed by understanding and applying the truth of propitiation; therefore, we need to
saturate our minds with passages of Scripture declaring God's love for
us.

I Corinthians 13 describes God's unconditional love for us. To
personalize this passage, replace the word "love" with "My Father."

Then, memorize the following passage and when fear comes, recall the love and kindness of God:

> My Father is very patient and kind.
> My Father is not envious, never boastful.
> My Father is not arrogant.
> My Father is never rude, nor is my Father self-seeking.
> My Father is not quick to take offense.
> He keeps no score of wrongs.
> My Father does not gloat over my sins, but is always glad when truth prevails.
> My Father knows no limit to His endurance, no end to His trust.
> My Father is always hopeful and patient.

As you memorize this passage, ask God to show you if your perception of Him is in error in any way. This will enable you to have a more accurate perception of God and will help to free you from the fear of punishment and the desire to punish others.

Chapter Seven

Shame

When past failures, dissatisfaction with personal appearance, or bad habits loom so large in our minds that they become the basis of our self-worth, the fourth false belief becomes established in our lives: *"I am what I am. I cannot change. I am hopeless."* This lie shackles people into the hopeless pessimism of poor self-esteem.

"I just can't help myself," some people say. "That's the way I've always been, and that's the way I'll always be. You can't teach an old dog new tricks." We assume that others should have low expectations of us, too. "You know I can't do any better than that. What do you expect?"

If we excuse our failures too often and for too long, we soon find our personality glued to them. Our self-image becomes no more than a reflection of the past.

When Leslie approached Janet about serving a term as president of the Ladies' Auxiliary, Janet fell apart.

"Are you serious?" she stuttered. "You know I've never been a leader or even gotten along well with people. No, no, I'd simply be an embarrassment to you. No, I couldn't do it, don't you see?"

Janet obviously suffered from low self-esteem. The opinions she held of herself were based on her failures of the past, and those failures now kept her from enjoying new experiences in her life.

A young man named Jeff once questioned me when I told him he needed to separate the past from the present, and that there was no natural law that dictated that he had to remain the same individual he had always been. I told Jeff that he could change, that he could rise above the past and build a new life for himself.

"But how can I do that?" Jeff asked. "I'm more of a realist than that. I know myself. I know what I've done and who I am. I've tried to change but it didn't work. I've given up now."

I explained to Jeff that he needed a new perspective, not just new efforts from the old, pessimistic perspective. He needed a new self-concept based on the unconditional love and acceptance of God. Both Jeff's past failures and God's unconditional love were realities, but the question was: Which one would Jeff value more? If he continued to value his failures, he would continue to be absorbed in self-pity. But if he would choose to study the truths of God's Word, memorize them, meditate on them, and tenaciously apply them, especially when he felt pessimistic, his sense of self-worth would change. Along with the change in self-worth would come changes in every area of his life: his goals, his relationships, and his outlook on life.

Too often our self-image rests solely on an evaluation of our past behavior, being measured only through a memory. Can you imagine buying stock from last month's Dow Jones report? Of course not, and yet, day after day, year after year, people build their personalities upon the rubble of yesterday's personal disappointments.

Perhaps we find some strange kind of comfort in our personal failings. Perhaps there is security in accepting ourselves as much less than we can become. That minimizes the risk of failure. Certainly the person who never expects much from himself will seldom be disappointed!

But nothing forces us to remain in the mold of the past. By the grace and power of God we can change! We can persevere and overcome! No one forces us to keep shifting our feet in the muck of old failures. We can dare to accept the challenge and build a new life.

Dr. Paul Tournier once compared life to a man hanging from a trapeze. The trapeze bar was the man's security, his pattern of existence, his lifestyle. Then God swung another trapeze into the man's view, and he faced a perplexing dilemma. Should he relinquish his past? Should he reach for the new bar?

The moment of truth came, Dr. Tournier explained, when the man realized that to grab onto the new bar, he must release the old one. If we choose to hang on tenaciously to the past, we will be unable to experience the joy, challenge, and yes, the potential for failure in the present. We must sever the past, throw ourselves out, and reach for change. Does this seem strange? Does it seem difficult? We may have difficulty relinquishing what is familiar (though painful) for what is unfamiliar because our fear of the unknown seems stronger than the pain of a poor self-concept. It seems right to hang on. Proverbs 16:25 says, *"There is a way which seems right to a man, but its end is the way of death."*

Any change in our behavior requires a release from our old self-concept, a concept often founded in failure and the expectations of others. We must relate to ourselves in a new way. To accomplish this, we must base our self-worth on God's opinion of us and trust in His Spirit to bring about change in our lives. Then, and only then, can we overcome Satan's deception that holds sway over our self-perception and behavior.

By believing Satan's lie: *"I am what I am, I cannot change, I am hopeless,"* we become vulnerable to pessimism and a poor self-concept. Take the test on the following page to determine how strongly you are affected by this false belief.

SHAME TEST

Read each statement. Look at the top of the test and choose the term which best describes your response. Put the number above that term in the blank beside the statement.

1	2	3	4	5	6	7
Always	Very Often	Often	Sometimes	Seldom	Very Seldom	Never

_____1.   I often think about past failures or experiences of rejection.

_____2.   There are certain things about my past which I cannot recall without experiencing strong, painful emotions (i.e., guilt, shame, anger, fear, etc.).

_____3.   I seem to make the same mistakes over and over again.

_____4.   There are certain aspects of my character I want to change, but don't believe I can ever successfully do so.

_____5.   I feel inferior.

_____6.   There are aspects of my appearance I cannot accept.

_____7.   I am generally disgusted with myself.

_____8.   I feel certain experiences have basically ruined my life.

_____9.   I perceive myself as an immoral person.

_____10.   I feel I have lost the opportunity to experience a complete and wonderful life.

_____ Total (Add up the numbers you have placed in the blanks.)

INTERPRETATION OF SCORE

If your score is...

57-70

God apparently has released you from the shame that plagues most people. The major exceptions to this are those who are either greatly deceived or have become callous to their own emotions as a way to suppress the pain.

47-56

Shame rarely or only in certain situations controls your experiences. Again, the only major exception involves those who are not honest with themselves.

37-46

When you experience emotional problems, they may relate to shame. In looking back, you can probably relate many of your decisions to this shame, and many of your decisions in the future will also be affected by low self-esteem unless you take direct action to overcome it.

27-36

Not only is the above category true of your experience, but shame forms a generally negative backdrop to your life. There are probably few days that you are not affected in some way by shame. Unfortunately, this also robs you of the joy and peace your salvation was meant to bring.

0-26

Experiences of shame dominate your memory, and have probably resulted in a great deal of depression. These problems will remain until some definitive action is taken. In other words, this condition will not simply disappear one day; time alone cannot heal your pain. You must deal with the root issue.

THE EFFECTS OF SHAME

Susan was the product of godless parents. Although she was a beautiful girl with dark brown eyes and long, silky hair, Susan never seemed quite as confident or outgoing as her brothers and sisters. One reason for this was that by her eighth birthday, Susan had been passed around among her father's friends for sexual favors. Overcome by the shame this caused her, Susan withdrew from others and looked for an escape.

By the time she was sixteen, Susan was addicted to alcohol and drugs, and was frequently stealing and selling her body for money. Susan had come to accept the fact that she was nothing more than sexual merchandise. Although she was ashamed of her lifestyle and wanted to change, she saw no way out. The only people who didn't seem to reject her were the same people who used her. She was not only ashamed, but also trapped and alone.

Unlike Susan, Diana was the product of Christian parents. She had been raised in a conservative Protestant church and was very active in the youth group. Diana was diligent in witnessing to her friends at school, and her actions were always an example to those around her.

However, one night Diana made a mistake that changed her life. Alone for the evening, she and her boyfriend went too far. Shocked and ashamed by their actions, they both agreed that they must admit the incident to their parents. Tearfully, Diana confided in her mother, looking for understanding and support. But Diana's mother lost control and bitterly told her how ashamed and disappointed she was. Diana's father couldn't believe what she had done, and he refused to even speak to her.

Her relationship with her parents continued to worsen and six months later, Diana left home. Heartbroken and overcome by shame, she turned to her boyfriend. Soon they began sleeping together regularly, and both began using drugs. Believing her parents would never accept her again, Diana sought acceptance in the only way she knew how.

Both Susan and Diana suffered the devastating effects of shame. It engulfs us when some flaw in our performance is so important, so overpowering, or so disappointing to us that it creates a permanently negative opinion about our self-worth. Others may not know of our failure, but we do. We may only imagine their rejection, but real or imagined, the pain from it cripples our confidence and hope.

Shame usually results in guilt and self-deprecation, but it can also lead us to search for God and His answers. Our inner, undeniable need for personal significance was created to make us search for Him who alone can fulfill our deep need. In Him, we find peace, acceptance, and love. Through Him, we find the courage and power to develop into the men and women He intends us to be. Although Satan wants to convince us that we will always be prisoners of our failures, and our past experiences, by God's grace we can be freed from our past and experience a renewed purpose for our lives.

Shame can have powerful effects on our lives, and it can manifest itself in many ways. Here is a brief list of some of the common problems associated with shame.

Inferiority

By definition, shame is a deep sense of inferiority. Feelings of inferiority can stem from only one or two haunting instances of failure, but they can destroy our self-worth, and as a result, adversely affect our emotions and behavior. Others may or may not actually believe we are inferior, but we must remember that God's opinion of us is vastly more important than our past failures or the opinions of others. Because of Christ's redemption, we are worthy, adequate, and complete in Him.

Habitually Destructive Behavior

It has been proven that we behave in a manner that is consistent with our perception of ourselves. Therefore, seeing ourselves through the eyes of shame will only result in more pessimism and a lifestyle of shameful acts.

Self-Pity

Shame often leads us to view ourselves as victims. As a result, we blame others for our actions as we sink into the depths of feeling sorry for ourselves.

Despising Our Appearance

In our society, beauty is of great value. In television commercials and programs, magazine ads, billboards, and almost everywhere we look, beauty is honored and valued. But very few of us compare to the beautiful people in the ads and programs, and most of us are ashamed of at least some aspect of our appearance. Billions of dollars and inestimable time and worry are spent in covering up or altering skin, eyes, noses, thighs, scalps, etc. We refuse to believe that God, in His sovereignty and love, gave us the features He wanted us to have.

GOD'S ANSWER: REGENERATION

Perhaps no passage in the Bible better illustrates God's regeneration than the story of Zaccheus in Luke 19:1-10. Zaccheus was a tax collector, despised by the people for overtaxing their meager earnings. There were few in the Roman world who were more despicable than tax collectors who got wealthy at others' expense. Yet one day, Zaccheus heard that Jesus was coming to his town, so he climbed up into a sycamore tree to get a better look at this man who reportedly loved even sinners and outcasts. Jesus saw him up in that tree and to the astonishment of all, including Zaccheus, Jesus went to Zaccheus' house to eat with him! At that dinner, Zaccheus' life was changed! He experienced the unconditional love and acceptance of Christ, and he became a different person. His self-concept was radically changed from a swindling, loathsome tax collector to a person who knew he was loved by God. His actions reflected this dramatic change. He pledged to repent of his sins and repay four-fold those he had swindled, and he also pledged to give half of his possessions to the poor. Zaccheus was a new person with new values, new goals, and new behavior.

How complete is our regeneration in Christ? It is so complete that nothing needs to be changed or improved upon. We are not accepted by God for what we are going to be, or for what we have been, but for who we are now in Christ. Ten thousand years of perfection in heaven will not make us even slightly more acceptable to God than we were the moment we trusted in Christ's payment for our sins.

Regeneration is not a self-improvement program, nor is it a clean-up campaign for our sinful natures. Regeneration is nothing less than the impartation of new life. As Paul stated in Ephesians 2:5, we were once dead in our sins, but we have been made alive in Christ. We are alive, forgiven, and complete in Christ!

The apostle Paul also wrote about this incredible transformation in his letter to the young pastor, Titus:

> *"For we also once were foolish ourselves, disobedient, deceived, enslaved to various lusts and pleasures, spending our life in malice and envy, hateful, hating one another. But when the kindness of God our Savior and His love for mankind appeared, He saved us, not on the basis of deeds which we have done in righteousness, but according to His mercy, by the washing of regeneration and renewing by the Holy Spirit, whom He poured out upon us richly through Jesus Christ our Savior, that being justified by His grace we might be made heirs according to the hope of eternal life"* (Titus 3:3-7).

Regeneration is the renewing work of the Holy Spirit that literally makes each believer a new person the instant he trusts Christ to be his Savior. In that wondrous, miraculous moment, we experience more than swapping one set of standards for another one. We experience regeneration, the impartation of new life. Jesus called it a new birth (John 3:3-6), a Spirit-wrought renewal of the human spirit, a transforming resuscitation which takes place so that *"the spirit is alive"* *(Romans 8:10).*

God has made us alive spiritually and made us complete. Paul wrote the Colossian Christians:

> *"For in Him (Christ) all the fullness of Deity dwells in bodily form, and in Him you have been made complete, and He is the head over all rule and authority" (Colossians 2:9, 10).*

In the church at Colossae, false teachers taught that "completeness" came through a combination of philosophy, good works, other religions, and Christ. Paul's clear message was that we are made complete through Christ alone. To attempt to find that completeness through any other sources, including success, the approval of others, prestige, or appearance, is to be taken captive through philosophy and empty deception. (Colossians 2:8) Nothing can add to the death of Christ to pay for our sins and the resurrection of Christ to give new life. We are complete because Christ has forgiven us and given us life – the capacity for change and growth.

One theologian remarked, "regeneration consists in the implanting of the principle of the new spiritual life in man, in a radical change of the governing disposition of the soul, which, under the influence of the Holy Spirit, gives birth to a life that moves in a Godward direction. In principle this change affects the whole man: the intellect . . . the will . . . and the feelings or emotions." (Louis Berkhof, Systematic Theology, p. 468)

When we trust Christ and experience new life, forgiveness, and love, we will see changes occur in our lives. Still, regeneration does not affect an instantaneous change in the total scope of our performance. We will still stumble and fall at times, but the Scriptures clearly instruct us to choose to act in ways that reflect our new lives and values in Christ:

> ". . . *lay aside the old self, which is being corrupted in accordance with the lusts of deceit, and that you be renewed in the spirit of your mind, and put on the new self, which in the likeness of God has been created in righteousness and holiness of the truth*" *(Ephesians 4:22-24).*

We are to put on this new self that progressively expresses Christian character in our attitudes and behavior. We are marvelously unique, and we can reflect the character of Christ through our individual personalities and behavior. Each believer, in a different and special way, has the capability to shine forth the light of God. No two will reflect His light in exactly the same way.

The truth of regeneration can dispel the specter of the past. Our sins have been forgiven, and we now have tremendous capabilities for growth and change because we are new people with the Spirit of God living in us. Yes, in sinning, we will experience the destructiveness of sin and the discipline of the Father, but sin does not change the truth of who we are in Christ.

To deal with our sin, we should follow King David's example. When Nathan confronted David about his sin of adultery with Bathsheba, David confessed his sin to the Lord (II Samuel 12:1-13). David did not run from his sin or the consequences resulting from it. David married Bathsheba, and God was merciful: He enabled Bathsheba to give birth to Solomon, the wise king of Israel. Certainly, God could have brought Solomon into the world some other way, but as a message to us, He chose Bathsheba. What a message! Confess your sins, get up, worship God, and get on with life. You can experience the mercy of God no matter what you've been through.

A BEGINNING EXERCISE

   Satan wants us to believe the lie: *"I am what I am. I cannot change. I am hopeless."* How can you be freed from the fear of shame? You can begin by looking up the following verses and reflecting on who you are in Christ. Beside each passage, write the truth about your new life in Christ.

   a.   Ephesians 2:10 -

   b.   Colossians 3:12 -

   c.   Matthew 5:13 -

   d.   I John 4:17 -

   e.   Ephesians 2:3 -

   f.   II Corinthians 5:21 -

   g.   Matthew 5:14 -

   h.   Romans 5: 17,18 -

   i.   Galatians 2:20 -

   j.   Romans 8:1 -

   k.   Ephesians 6:10 -

   l.   Romans 8:37 -

   m.   Colossians 2:10 -

n.   Romans 8:17 -

o.   Romans 1:7 -

p.   Ephesians 1:6 -

q.   I Peter 1:16 -

r.   II Corinthians 5:17 -

s.   Ephesians 1:7 -

To summarize the last four chapters:

Because of justification, you are completely forgiven and fully pleasing to God. You no longer have to fear failure.

Because of reconciliation, you are totally accepted by God. You no longer have to fear rejection.

Because of propitiation, you are deeply loved by God. You no longer have to fear punishment or have to punish others.

Because of regeneration, you have been made brana new, complete in Christ. You no longer need to experience the pain of shame.

Chapter Eight

Summarizing the Search

In order to summarize mankind's search for significance, we need to answer one important question: When he had the rest of the uninhabited world to enjoy, why was Satan determined to enslave Adam and Eve, two seemingly insignificant beings?

To begin with, Satan probably desired to enslave them because he sought revenge against God who dispelled him and his followers from heaven and cast them down from a position of great power. Satan may have thought that the best way to get revenge was to thwart God's plan for His prized creation --- man. Since Adam and Eve were created to bear the image of God and to give Him true worship and companionship, Satan believed that corrupting them and turning them away from their Creator would spoil God's plan.

Also, Satan may have tried to enslave Adam and Eve in an effort to gain control over the earth. Adam and Eve were authorized to rule over the earth (Genesis 1:28-30). God had given them dominion over all the works of His hands, all the sheep and oxen, the birds of the air, the fish of the sea, and all the vegetation that grew under heaven. Therefore, being cast out of heaven and down to earth, Satan found himself exiled as a tenant on a planet God had given to man. As the archangel Lucifer, Satan was once free to walk in and out of the very presence of God. But now, Satan was confined to an earth that he did not control. Adam's right to rule was granted by God, and Satan could not snatch that authority away from him. Therefore, Satan's only chance to gain control and thwart the plan of God was to turn mankind against God and to trick Adam into willingly giving his authority to him.

Did Satan succeed? On first examination, we would probably answer, yes. However, the Bible tells us that Adam was not deceived by Satan's subtle lies (I Timothy 2:14). No, Adam deliberately chose to disobey God. In his rebellion against God, Adam chose to obey Satan's desires, and in doing so, found himself enslaved to Satan. Because the owner of a slave owns all the slave possesses, Satan took over the earth. Adam committed the sin His Creator had specifically warned him about: the sin of rebellion against God. There could be no instant restoration to perfection. When Adam squandered away his rights and dominion, Satan became the god of this world (II Corinthians 4:4), the ruler of this world, the prince of the power of the air (Ephesians 2:1-3).

As a result, man's intellectual and spiritual eyes became darkened, and his mind was filled with pride and vain imaginations. Created in the image of God, man now became the slave of Satan, destined to live in the curse of disease, pain, and death. Rejecting the authority of God, Adam sold us into slavery to sin, and we became enemies of God, deserving the righteous wrath of Almighty God.

And yet, there is recourse. God has left open the door to life through Christ's death and resurrection. God's anger can be turned away from us if we trust in Christ's death on the cross to pay the penalty for our sin. Instead of being His enemies, we can be reconciled to God and become His friends, eager to honor Him.

Our redemption was made complete at Calvary. In John 19:30, when Jesus lifted up His eyes and cried, *"It is finished!"* He told us that the provision for reconciliation was complete. Nothing more needed to be done, because the word of life had been spoken to all mankind. We needed only to hear the word and accept it, placing our hope and trust in Christ.

But if the redemption we enjoy is complete, why do we so often fail to see the fruit we long for? Why do we wrestle day after day with the same temptations, the same failings, the same distractions we have fought so long? Why can't we break free and move on toward maturity? Christ illustrated the reasons for a lack of fruitfulness in the parable of the sower in Mark 4:1-20. Productivity is dependent on the fertility of the soil and the presence or absence of weeds. The reasons Christ gave for a lack of fruit were: Satan taking away the Word of God, persecution, and the worries of the world. For the vast majority of us, the worries of the world constitute the major culprit for our lack of fruitfulness. Jesus describes it this way:

> *"And others are the ones on whom the seed was sown among the thorns; these are the ones who have heard the word, and the worries of the world, and the deceitfulness of riches, and the desires for other things enter in and choke the word, and it becomes unfruitful" (Mark 4:18, 19).*

We need to focus on the forgiveness we have received and reject the deception and worldly desires that choke out the word of life. We must base our lives on God's Word and allow His character to be reproduced within us by the power of His Spirit:

> *"And those are the ones on whom seed was sown on the good soil; and they hear the word and accept it, and bear fruit, thirty, sixty, and a hundred-fold" (Mark 4:20).*

The moment we trust Christ, we are given *"everything pertaining to life and godliness" (II Peter 1:2-4).* Immediately we become His sons and daughters, with all the provisions He has graciously given us. As we allow Him to reign over the affairs of our lives, He transforms our values, attitudes, and behavior so that we are able to glorify Him more and more. Of course, we are still chained to a mortal body, but we are reborn in righteousness and holiness of the truth. We have within us the Christ who has authority over Satan. Christ has triumphed over him by the power of His death to pay for sin and by the power of His resurrection to give new life (Colossians 2:15).

Now redeemed, we can only be denied our rightful purpose to rule in life if we continue to be deceived by Satan. If we fail to recognize our true position of sonship and let our new power and authority go unused, we will remain mired in the world's system. Satan's lies and schemes are designed to keep us from recognizing and experiencing these wonderful truths.

In order to overcome Satan's lies and free ourselves from these false beliefs we need to have a clear understanding of what Christ has done for us through His death at Calvary. The more we realize the implications of the cross, the more we will experience the freedom, motivation, and power God intends for us. God's Word is the source of truth - the truth about Christ, the cross, and redemption. The cross is not just the beginning of the Christian life, it is our constant motivation to grow spiritually and to live for Christ:

> *"Now for this very reason also, applying all diligence, in your faith supply moral excellence, and in your moral excellence, knowledge; And in your knowledge, self-control, and in your self-control, perseverance, and in your perseverance, godliness; And in your godliness, brotherly kindness, and in your brotherly kindness, Christian love. For if these qualities are yours and are increasing, they render you neither useless nor unfruitful in the true knowledge of our Lord Jesus Christ. For he who lacks these qualities is blind or shortsighted,*

having forgotten his purification from his former sins"
(II Peter 1:5-9).

This passage clearly teaches that the absence of spiritual growth can be traced to a lack of understanding or a failure to remember the implications of the forgiveness of Christ. The cross is central to our motivation and development.

I have given you a beginning exercise for each false belief, but this is only a start. In the closing chapters we'll look at the basics of renewing the heart and mind: experiencing the power of the Holy Spirit and replacing thought patterns that tell us our worth is based on our performance plus others' opinions with thought patterns that focus on the truths of God's unconditional love for us.

Let's review for a minute. The chart on the following pages depicts the contrast between the rival belief systems. Use the chart to help determine if any particular thought is based on a lie or on God's truth. If the thought is based on a lie, confront it and overcome it with the truth of God's Word.

FALSE BELIEFS	CONSEQUENCES OF FALSE BELIEFS
I must meet certain standards in order to feel good about myself.	The fear of failure; perfectionism; intensity about your own success; withdrawal from risks; manipulate others to help you succeed.
I must have the approval of certain others to feel good about myself.	The fear of rejection; please others at any cost; sensitive to criticism, withdrawal to avoid disapproval.
Those who fail are unworthy of love and deserve to be punished.	The fear of punishment; punishing others; blame others when you fail; dry spiritual life.
I am what I am. I cannot change. I am hopeless.	Inferiority feelings; destructive habits; hopelessness.

GOD'S SPECIFIC SOLUTION	RESULTS OF GOD'S SOLUTION
Because of justification, we are completely forgiven and fully pleasing to God. We no longer have to fear failure.	Freedom from the fear of failure; intensity about the right things: Christ and His Kingdom; love for Christ.
Because of reconciliation, we are totally accepted by God. We no longer have to fear rejection.	Freedom from the fear of rejection; willingness to be open and vulnerable; able to relax around others; willingness to take criticism; desire to please God no matter what others think.
Because of propitiation, we are deeply loved by God. We no longer have to fear punishment or punish others.	Freedom from the fear of punishment; patience and kindness toward others; being quick to forgive; deep love for Christ.
Because of regeneration, we have been made brand new, complete in Christ. We no longer need to experience the pain of shame.	Christ-centered self-confidence; joy, courage, peace; desire to know Christ.

Chapter Nine

The Holy Spirit ---
The Source of Change

The truths we have examined in this book have tremendous implications in every relationship and every goal in our lives, but now the question arises, how do we actually implement these truths? How do the changes actually take place? Jesus supplied the answer to this question in His last time of intimate instruction with His disciples (John 13-16). Jesus told His disciples that He would soon be put to death, but they would not be left alone. *"And I will ask the Father, and He will give you another Helper, that He may be with you forever" (John 14:16).* That Helper is the Holy Spirit, who came some 50 days later to direct and empower the believers at Pentecost. That same Holy Spirit indwells each believer today and serves as our instructor, counselor, and source of spiritual power as we live for Christ's glory and honor.

Who is the Holy Spirit, and why did He come? The Holy Spirit, the third person of the Trinity, is God and possesses all the attributes of deity. The Holy Spirit's primary purpose is to glorify Christ and bring attention to Him. Christ said, *"He shall glorify Me; for He shall take of Mine, and shall disclose it to you" (John 16:54).* The Holy Spirit is our teacher and He guides us into the truth of the Scriptures (John 16:13). It is by His power that the love of Christ flows through us and produces spiritual fruit (John 7:37-39, 15:1-8). This spiritual fruit is described in many ways in the New Testament including: intimate friendship with Christ (John 15:14), love for one another (John 15:12), joy and peace in the midst of difficulties (John 14:27, 15:11), steadfastness (I Corinthians 15:58), self-control, singing, thankfulness, and submission (Ephesians 5:18-21), and evangelism and discipleship (Matthew 28:18-20).

Obviously, this fruit is not always evident in the lives of Christians, but why not? As we all know, the Christian life is not an easy one. It is not simply a self-improvement program. True, we may be able at times to make some changes in our habits through our own discipline and determination, but Christianity is not merely self-effort. The Christian life is a supernatural life in which we draw on Christ as our resource for direction, encouragement, and strength. In one of the most widely known metaphors of the Bible, Christ described the Christian life in John 15 with the illustration of a branch and a vine. He said:

> *"I am the true vine, and My Father is the vine dresser....Abide in* (live, grow, and gain your sustenance from) *Me, and I in you. As the branch cannot bear fruit of itself, unless it abides in the vine, so neither can you, unless you abide in Me. I am the vine, you are the branches; he who abides in Me, and I in him, he bears much fruit; for apart from Me you can do nothing" (John 15:1,4,5).*

Nothing? Yes, in terms of that which is honoring to Christ, spiritually nourishing to you, and genuine Christian service, anything done apart from the love and power of Christ amounts to nothing. Although there may have been tremendous personal effort expended and great cost involved, only that which is done for Christ's glory and in the power of His Spirit is of eternal value. However, the very power of God that was evident when Christ was raised from the dead (Ephesians 1:19-21) is available to the believer who abides in Christ, desiring that He be honored and trusting that His Spirit will produce fruit in his life.

Just as the cross of Christ is the basis of our relationship with God, it is also the foundation of our spiritual growth. The death of Christ is the supreme demonstration of the love, power, and wisdom of God, and the more we understand and apply the truths of justification, propitiation, reconciliation, and regeneration, the more our lives will reflect the character of Christ. Spiritual growth is not magic. It comes as we apply the love and forgiveness of Christ in our daily circumstances --- reflecting on the unconditional acceptance of Christ and His awesome power, and choosing to respond to situations and people in light of His sovereign purpose and kindness toward us. As we saw in the previous chapter, the apostle Peter stated very clearly that our forgiveness bought by the death of Christ is the foundation of spiritual growth:

> "Now for this very reason also, applying all diligence, in your faith supply moral excellence, and in your moral excellence, knowledge; and in your knowledge, self-control, and in your self-control, perseverance, and in your perseverance, godliness; and in your godliness, brotherly kindness, and in your brotherly kindness, love. For if these qualities are yours and are increasing, they render you neither useless nor unfruitful in the true knowledge of our Lord Jesus Christ. For he who lacks these qualities is blind or shortsighted, having forgotten his purification from his former sins" (II Peter 1:5-9).

The clear implication from this passage is that the absence of spiritual growth signifies a lack of understanding of forgiveness. Seeking an emotional experience, going to seminar after seminar, or looking for a "deeper life" is not the solution. Emotional experiences, seminars, and studies are only valid if their foundation is the love, forgiveness, and power of the cross and resurrection of Christ. There is nothing more motivating, nothing more comforting, nothing else that compels us more to honor Christ, and nothing else that gives us as much compassion for others as the sacrificial payment of Christ to rescue us from eternal condemnation.

The primary reason that Christians don't experience a deep and fruitful relationship with Christ is that they do not grasp the significance of their forgiveness. Yet there are several variations of this reason that are instructive for us to examine. Christians face five obstacles that stem from a misunderstanding of Christ's love and forgiveness:

1. They have wrong purposes.
2. They are too mechanical in their approach to the Christian life.
3. They are too mystical.
4. They lack knowledge about Christ's love and power available to them.
5. They are harboring sin which blocks their fellowship with Christ.

Let's take a closer look at these five obstacles. First of all, many Christians have wrong purposes in living the Christian life. Although their actions and words may appear sincere, many are desiring to honor themselves rather than Christ. Some may be blatant pleasure-seekers, while others may be deeply involved in Christian service but with wrong motives; however, their intentions are the same -- to be successful and gain the approval of others. Yet the Lord will not share His glory with another because He alone deserves honor and praise. If we realize that our needs for security and approval are fully met in

Christ, we will be able to take our attention and affections off of ourselves and place them on Christ. Only then can we develop Paul's intense desire to honor Christ: *"Therefore also we have as our ambi-
tion...to be pleasing to Him"* (II Corinthians 5:9).

Personal success and pleasing others are obviously improper
goals for Christians, but there is another improper goal that is much
more subtle and deceptive: spiritual growth. Fruitfulness and growth
are the results of focusing on Christ and desiring to honor Him. They
are not the goal. When spiritual growth is the goal of a person's life,
he tends to be preoccupied with himself instead of Christ: "Am I
growing? Am I more like Christ today? What am I learning?" This in-
ordinate preoccupation with self-improvement parallels our culture's
self-help and personal enhancement movement in many ways. Personal development is certainly not wrong, but it is wrong to make it a
pre-eminent goal. If it is a goal at all, it should be a secondary one.
Honoring Christ should be our consuming passion. God wants us to
have a healthy self-awareness and to periodically analyze our lives, but
He does not want us to be preoccupied with ourselves. The only One
worth our preoccupation is Christ. Furthermore, we will grow much
more if we take our attention off of our development and fruitfulness
(or lack thereof) and focus on the love, power, and wisdom of Christ.
Our goal is clear: to honor Him because He is worthy.

Secondly, some believers are too mechanical in their approach
to the Christian life. Although they rigorously schedule and discipline
their lives in an effort to conform to what they believe is a Biblical lifestyle, their lives exhibit little of the freshness, joy, and spontaneity of
Christ. One man had organized his life into hourly segments, each
designated to accomplish some particular "Biblical purpose." True, he
was organized and accomplished some good things, but he was
miserable. This man was trusting in himself instead of the Holy Spirit
to produce a life that pleased God. When he realized that Christ said
that the foremost commandment is to love Him and others (Matthew
22:36-39), and that joy, peace, and kindness are much more important

than adhering to strict rules (for which Jesus rebuked the Pharisees), he took on a new perspective and a new lifestyle of love and joy. This man still was an organized person, but being organized no longer dominated his life. Though we may not be that extreme, many of us do have certain Christian activities (church attendance, tithing, Bible studies, etc.) that we feel we must perform to be "good Christians." These activities themselves are obviously not wrong, but that perspective is wrong. Christ wants us to receive our joy and acceptance from Him instead of merely following rules or schedules. He is the Lord; He alone is our source of security, joy, and meaning.

A third obstacle to abiding in Christ is that many believers become too mystical, looking for some supernatural feeling in their relationship. This dependence on feelings leads to two problems. The first one occurs when a person waits for feelings to motivate him, while in the other, the person sees virtually every emotion as a sign from God. Let's examine these.

Some Christians do not get up in the morning until "the Lord tells them to." They don't want to share Christ with people until they "feel" like God is prompting them. What these Christians are forgetting is that Christianity is primarily faith in action. Our emotions are not the most reliable source of motivation. Yes, the Holy Spirit does motivate and empower us, but He has already instructed us through the Scriptures with the vast majority of what He wants us to do. Rather than waiting for a "holy zap" to get us going, we need to believe the truth of God's Word and take action for His glory. Must we wait until we feel like God wants us to love other Christians, pray, study the Scriptures, share our faith, or serve His cause? No! We need to follow the examples recounted in Hebrews 11 of the men and women who acted on their faith in God, often in spite of their feelings. True, these people were often reflective and prayed about what God wanted them to do, but they always acted on the truth of God.

The second problem of dependence on feelings is the other extreme. It occurs when people believe that their emotions are a primary means of God's communication with them, and therefore, their feelings are understood as signs from God to indicate His leading. This conclusion often leads them to make authoritative statements about God's will (for both themselves and others) that are based on no more than how they feel. As in the first extreme, the Scriptures are forced to take a back seat as even foolish and immoral acts are justified by this false "leading from the Lord."

Our society glorifies pleasant feelings, and all of us are affected by this to some degree. We are told that we deserve to be happy, to be comfortable, to be loved, and to be stimulated, but instead, living by our feelings brings frustration, mood swings, self-centeredness, and spiritual immobility. It may come as a shock to some people, but happiness is not the goal of the Christian life! Our goal is to glorify Christ, and we can do that as an act of the will, even in spite of our feelings.

The Scriptures never tell us to live by our emotions. "If it feels good, do it!" is not a verse from the Bible! The truths of the Scriptures are the only reliable guide for our lives. Our feelings may reinforce these truths, but they may reflect just the opposite, telling us that God doesn't love us, that the fun of a particular sin is more satisfying than following God, or that God will never answer our prayers. The truth of God's Word is our authority, not our feelings.

Does this mean we should repress our feelings or deny that we have them? No, we should acknowledge them to the Lord, fully express to Him how we feel, and look at the Scriptures to determine what He would have us do. Then, in obedience to the Word of God, whether we feel like it or not, we should do what honors Christ. Many times when we obey Christ in spite of our feelings, the emotion of joy and peace follows sooner or later.

It is not wrong to have emotions, but we need to go beyond feelings to determine God's leading in our lives. We need to develop a blend of a proper understanding of the Scriptures and a sensitivity to His Spirit. God's Word is our ultimate authority, and we need to be good students of it so we will understand the character and will of God. As Paul told Timothy:

> "*All Scripture is inspired by God and profitable for teaching, for reproof, for correction, and for training in righteousness, that the man of God may be adequate, equipped for every good work*" (*II Timothy 3:16, 17*).

We also need to develop a sensitivity to the Holy Spirit that goes beyond raw emotions. This sensitivity is an awareness of His conviction of sin, His leading to be kind to another person, His prompting to share the gospel, etc. These Spirit-induced impressions may correspond with what we want to do, but instead, they may be antithetical to what we feel like doing. The discernment of whether the impression is of God or not comes from two primary sources: the clear teaching of the Scriptures and previous experiences of learning to discern the leading of the Holy Spirit. If an impression is from God, it will not violate Biblical principles. Also, a person who has developed the habit of being sensitive to God is more likely to accurately discern the leading of God than someone who is just beginning to develop a sensitivity to the Lord.

One of the most helpful activities for developing a moment by moment awareness of God is thankfulness. Complaining may be much easier and more natural, but it hardly focuses our attention on Christ! Being thankful even in the midst of difficulties rivets our attention on the Lord and enables us to see His wisdom, sovereignty, power, and love. That makes us more conscious of His character and purposes, it promotes prayer, and it makes us more sensitive to His Spirit's prompting.

Fourthly, many Christians are hindered in their walk with God because they do not realize the nature of the love and power available in Christ. They haven't yet learned the magnificent truths of the Scriptures -- *that we are deeply loved, totally forgiven, fully pleasing, totally accepted, and complete in Christ,* with all the power of the resurrection available to us. These believers are like the West Texas sheep rancher who lived in poverty even though vast resources of oil were under his property. He was fabulously rich, but he didn't even know it. Since it was discovered, many years ago, the Yates oil field has proven to be one of the richest and most productive in the world. Similarly, we have incredible resources available to us, and we are rich in the love and power of God. We need only to study the Scriptures and recognize all that is available to us through Christ's great love and power.

The Holy Spirit enables us to experience the reality of Christ's love and power in many ways, including:

-- revealing sin in our lives so that we can confess it and our fellowship with God won't be hindered (I John 1:9);

-- helping us choose to honor Christ in our circumstances and relationships (II Corinthians 5:9);

-- enabling us to endure as we follow Christ (Romans 5:1-5);

-- producing fruit in us (Galatians 5:22, 23; John 15:1-8).

Willful sin is a fifth obstacle that clouds many Christians' fellowship with God. Indeed, sin may be pleasurable for a moment, but inevitably its destructive nature will reveal itself in many ways -- broken relationships, poor self-esteem, and a poor witness for Christ. Whether it is a gross sin of immorality or the more subtle sin of pride, all sin must be dealt with decisively. Christ's death paid for all our sins and they are completely forgiven.

We need to admit that we have sinned and claim the forgiveness of Christ for any and every sin immediately after the sin occurs, so that our fellowship with Christ will be unhindered, and we can continue to experience His love and power.

Paul wrote to the Galatian Christians:

"The fruit of the Spirit is love, joy, peace, patience, kindness, goodness, faithfulness, gentleness, and self-control...." *(Galatians 5:22, 23).*

As we respond to the love of Christ and trust His Spirit to fill us, then these characteristics will become increasingly evident in our lives. The filling of the Holy Spirit includes two major aspects: our purpose (to bring honor to Christ instead of ourselves) and our resources (trusting in His love and power to accomplish results instead of trusting in our own wisdom and abilities). Although we will continue to mature in our relationship with the Lord over the years, we can begin to experience His love, strength, and purpose from the moment we put Him at the center of our lives.

Spencer, a junior at the University of Missouri, had been a Christian for several years. He accepted Christ as his personal Savior when a friend from his dorm shared the gospel with him during his first semester at the university. Although he began consistently growing in his relationship with Christ, intramural athletics and parties with his rowdy friends had become the focus of Spencer's life by the middle of his sophomore year. Spencer still went to church frequently, and occasionally he even went to Christian meetings on campus, but he was confused and often felt guilty about his friends and the activities they were involved in. He tried talking with his friends about it, but they only laughed. Although he wasn't very comfortable with these friends anymore, Spencer felt like he needed them and continued spending time with them.

Then, in the fall of his junior year, Spencer went to several Christian meetings on campus. He began hearing about the love and power of Christ and how the Holy Spirit can enable us to live for Christ. Through this teaching, Spencer also began to develop an eternal perspective, recognizing that worldliness and sin are destructive, but that following Christ is eternally significant. One night, Spencer spent some time alone praying and thinking about what he had learned. He realized that his life was confusing and frustrating, and dishonoring to the Lord. Spencer also realized that Christ is worthy of his love and obedience, so he decided to live for Him. As he began to confess the specific sins the Holy Spirit brought to his mind and ask Him for the power to live in a way that was pleasing to Christ, Spencer felt relief and joy -- he was doing the right thing. But what about his friends? Spencer decided to continue getting strong Christian teaching and fellowship, and he also planned to tell his friends about his decision to follow Christ. Some of his friends laughed, others were surprised, and a few were even angry. Over the next year, Spencer still spent some time with these friends, but now at ball games instead of wild parties. He even shared Christ with most of them and had the joy of seeing two of them trust Christ. Spencer had his share of struggles and spiritual growing pains, but he had a new consistency, purpose, and thankfulness to the Lord.

Like Spencer, our own willingness to be filled with the Holy Spirit is a direct response to the magnificent truths centered in the cross and resurrection of Christ: *We are deeply loved by God, completely forgiven and fully pleasing to God, totally accepted by God, and complete in Him.* Are you depending on God's Spirit to teach you, change you, and use you in the lives of others? If so, keep on trusting Him! If not, look over the five obstacles to following Christ and see if any of these are obstructing your relationship with Him. Are there specific sins you need to confess? Confession means "to agree" with God that you have sinned and that Christ has completely forgiven you. It also means to repent, to turn from your sin to a life of love and obedience to God.

Take the time to reflect on the love and power of Christ and decide to trust Him to guide you by His Word, fill you with His Spirit, and enable you to live for Him and be used in the lives of others. Abiding in Christ does not take away all your problems, but it provides a powerful relationship with the One who is the source of wisdom to help you make difficult decisions, love to encourage you, and strength to help you endure.

Chapter Ten

Renewing the Mind

In one of the most famous dialogues in the Bible, Jesus explained the profound truth of regeneration to Nicodemus:

> *"...unless one is born again, he cannot see the kingdom of God... That which is born of the flesh is flesh, and that which is born of the Spirit is spirit. Do not marvel that I said to you, 'You must be born again'" (John 3:3,6,7).*

When we were born, we entered a world ruled by Satan, and we learned the ways of the world. *"You are of your father the devil,"* Jesus explained, *"and you want to do the desires of your father"* (John 8:44). Therefore, it is easy to understand why we believe Satan's lies so readily!

However, at some point in our lives the Holy Spirit drew us to Christ, and we trusted Him to forgive us and give us new purpose and meaning. The Holy Spirit baptized us into the body of Christ, a new spiritual family, the family of God. He plucked us from the family of Satan and adopted us into God's eternal family as sons and daughters

(Colossians 1:13,14; Romans 8:15). We were cursed to die as members of Satan's family, but as members of God's family, we have been granted everything pertaining to life and godliness from the very moment of our new birth. We were not forced to qualify to receive God's provisions, but instead, we receive the rights and privileges of sons by the grace and mercy of God.

If an earthly father receives his newborn son into his arms and lavishes the child with good things, how much more does our Heavenly Father lavish upon His children? When we are born into an earthly family, we are given a name, all the provisions of food, clothing, and shelter to sustain us, and perhaps even made the beneficiary of a savings account for our future. All the abilities of the father to provide for the child begin to work on the child's behalf before he has yet to perform well or badly. The child is bound to his earthly father by the unconditional right of birth, not by his ability to perform.

So much more so are newly born children of God bound to their Heavenly Father. As His children, we are given a new spirit, endowed with the Holy Spirit to lead and convict us, and given all the capability to honor God and live purposeful and meaningful lives. All His provisions become ours at our spiritual birth before we do good or evil.

And yet, as babes we are not mature. We need to grow and progress, taking on the characteristics of our Heavenly Father. We may rebel, but He is long suffering and capable of loving correction and instruction. We may fail Him, but we are still His children.

It is interesting that when the Holy Spirit gave us a new spirit, He did not give us a totally renewed mind. Although we have the Spirit of Christ living within us to enable us to evaluate our experiences, our minds tend to dwell on the worldly thoughts of our old nature instead of on God's truth. As babes in Christ, we are children in conflict, torn between the new godly motivation to glorify Christ and the old motivations of lust and pride. Paul recognized that conflict. He wrote the Christians in Rome:

"I find then the principle that evil is present in me, the one who wishes to do good. For I joyfully concur with the law of God in the inner man, but I see a different law in the members of my body, waging war against the law of my mind, and making me a prisoner of the law of sin which is in my members. Wretched man that I am! Who will set me free from the body of this death? Thanks be to God through Jesus Christ our Lord!. . ." (Romans 7:21-25).

How then can we break free from the law of sin and begin to grow in Christ? How can we assist the process that will enable us to follow Christ? To change our behavior, we must reject the earthly thoughts and replace them with spiritual thoughts. Solomon said, *"As a man thinks within himself, so he is" (Proverbs 23:7).* Therefore, the way we think affects the way we feel, the way we perceive ourselves and others, and ultimately, the way we act. The way we think determines whether we will live according to God's truth or the world's value system. Still writing to the Christians in Rome, Paul explains the serious implications of how we think:

"And do not be conformed to this world, but be transformed by the renewing of your mind, that you may prove what the will of God is, that which is good and acceptable and perfect" (Romans 12:2).

We interpret every activity and circumstance around us through our beliefs. Some of these interpretations are conscious reflections; however, most of them are based on unconscious assumptions. It is from these conscious and unconscious interpretations we react and respond. The following diagram will aid in understanding this process. The situations we encounter are interpreted through our beliefs.

These beliefs trigger certain thoughts, which in turn stimulate certain emotions, and from these emotions come our actions.

Situations

Beliefs ⇨ Thoughts ⇨ Emotions ⇨ Actions

Again, thoughts result from beliefs and then these thoughts trigger our emotions. However, in order for an emotion to persist, the belief system must continue to produce certain thoughts. For example, you cannot stay sad without continuing to think sad thoughts. Think of it in this way: A person's mind contains deeply held beliefs and attitudes which have been learned through environment, experiences, and education. These beliefs and attitudes produce thoughts which reflect how we perceive the events in our lives. These thoughts, then, are the source of our emotions, and emotions are the launching pad for actions.

The understanding that thoughts are products of beliefs gives us a tool for exposing them. Then we can identify the source of those beliefs. Which false belief do the following thoughts expose?

1.   He just has to like me.
2.   What can I do to make him like me more?
3.   I'm afraid he's given up on me.

These thoughts reveal a belief in Satan's lie that we must be approved by certain people to have self-worth. In this same manner, all of our thoughts can be traced back to beliefs -- beliefs either based on the truths of Scripture or the lies of Satan.

False beliefs can be deceptive because they may be based on a partially accurate perception of circumstances. For example, it may be accurate that you failed to get a report in on time. You did actually fail, but that is only part of the truth. The other part is that your self-worth is not affected by that failure. To recognize your failure, but then believe that your failure has caused you to lose self-worth, is to believe both a truth and a lie. The facts may be true, but our interpretation of the facts may be based on the crafty deceit of Satan.

Also, in many cases an accurate perception may trigger a whole array of unconscious thoughts stemming from false beliefs. For example, Kay's accurate perception, "My husband is drinking again," actually represents many of the following unconscious thoughts:

"I hate that inconsiderate bum!"

"He'll start mistreating me and the children."

"I'll finally have to move out."

"I'll be forced to provide for myself and the children."

"I don't have any skills that qualify me to earn a living."

"I'm nothing but a failure."

Kay was responding emotionally not only to the conscious thought of her husband's drinking, but to unconscious fears as well. The combination of the accurate perceptions and speculative assumptions formed a mental framework which spawned her emotions and actions. Therefore, we need to analyze our thoughts in each circumstance to determine which are valid and which are not.

In addition, we often prolong destructive emotions by continuing to dwell on them. This is illustrated by Samantha, who lost her temper with the grocery boy for spilling a sack of vegetables on the parking lot. Later that night, Samantha was still angry. "The more I think about it, the more angry I get," she told her husband.

"So don't think about it," he calmly replied.

In this situation, Samantha was wrong on two counts. First, she let her emotions dictate her angry response to the grocery boy. Secondly, she let her thoughts cloud her emotions, which robbed her of joy. Her negative actions, thoughts, and emotions then reinforced one another, and her anger was solidified.

The example is a simple one, but the point is clear: The way we believe and think determines how we react to the world around us. If our minds have not been renewed by the power of Christ, it is impossible to display His character in these daily situations.

For most of us, the majority of our beliefs were produced before we became Christians; therefore, it is easy to understand why many of our actions do not reflect His character. Until those false beliefs are identified, ruthlessly rooted out, and replaced with Biblical convictions, our lives will continue to be filled with dishonorable thoughts and actions. Since these false beliefs are contradictory to the Word of God, we can conclude that the very pillars of thought which have shaped our personalities are in error and at odds with God's truth. Failure to recognize this fact can have devastating effects on our lives.

For example, a young girl named Dawn was sent to me by her parents who hoped I could reason with her about her promiscuous behavior. But Dawn could not understand how something that felt so good and made her so happy could be wrong. In an effort to explain, I pointed out that her pleasant emotions were not the ultimate determination of truth. Emotions can be very misleading. I urged Dawn to realize the destructiveness of her sin, and I explained how God could meet her needs. I also explained to her that she was increasingly in bondage to her sin even though she was enjoying it. Dawn could be freed from her sin and its destructive effects. It was a clear choice: to continue to follow her emotions, or to believe the truth of God's Word and experience true and lasting joy instead of a destructive counterfeit.

Our emotions are born from our beliefs about a situation, not the situation itself. Therefore, it is crucial to readjust our beliefs, instead of trying to escape our situations. Jack, a middle aged executive, is a perfect example of this truth. When Jack told me that he had lost his job and was depressed, he meant that an event (the loss of his job) had caused his sadness and depression. To teach him that events don't cause emotions, I pretended to miss the correlation.

"Why are you depressed?" I asked.

"I lost my job, and I feel depressed," Jack stated.

"I heard that, but why are you depressed?," I repeated.

Jack bristled. "What! I told you I'm depressed because I lost my job."

"No, your job isn't why you're depressed," I reasoned. "This morning a man told me that although he had lost his job, he was excited about seeing what God would provide. Why is it that what causes depression in one person causes excitement in another?"

"I don't know," Jack replied thoughtfully.

"The reason," I went on to explain, "is that our emotions are a result of our beliefs about a situation, not the situation itself. Because circumstances themselves do not cause emotions, we must entrust the circumstances to God and focus on our beliefs, making sure they line up with the truths of the Bible. This way, we can be secure and happy - - even when the job runs out! Who knows where God plans to take you next?!"

Finally, Jack could better understand how God was working in his life.

The case of Winston also provides a clear example of how we can gain victory over our circumstances and emotions. Winston was an older man with only a few years left until retirement. But Winston had become particularly anxious since he had a new boss who assigned him degrading tasks, seemingly designed to run him off. The pressure upset Winston so much he seriously considered an early retirement. Winston came to me for advice and explained the situation carefully. He was shocked when I told him his problem wasn't the new boss, but rather, the way he perceived the situation.

"What!" Winston sputtered. "Are you trying to tell me after all this, that my problem is not my situation? Are you saying the awful way I am being treated isn't really what's making me feel depressed?"

"Precisely," I said. "Your anxiety comes from your false belief about yourself."

I began explaining to Winston that he was operating with a false belief that he must be approved by his boss in order to be happy. I further pointed out that God was probably allowing this situation to free him from being dependent on the approval of anyone. Then he could experience what really mattered in life: that *he was deeply loved by God, completely forgiven, fully pleasing, totally accepted, and complete in Christ*, resulting in a life of love and depth and meaning.

"Why worry about your boss' evaluation of you?" I said. "It is only what Christ thinks about you that really matters. You can let those degrading tasks come and go without getting upset if you value His acceptance of you more than your boss' apparent rejection."

Smiling, Winston went back to work, determined to replace the false belief with the truth of reconciliation. Later Winston told me that his boss quit pressuring him when he realized that assigning him degrading tasks no longer disturbed him.

One of the greatest characteristics of personal maturity in Christ is the willingness to accept full responsibility for our emotional and behavioral reactions in all the disturbing situations of life. In realizing our situations don't cause our self-destructive reactions and by applying God's truths to the situation, we find peace and perspective.

The world need not have control over God's children. The spiritual battle may be intense, but we will be able to persevere if we analyze our circumstances through God's perspective and reject the false beliefs which can control our emotions and actions. Faith in the Word of God prevents us from being buffeted by every situation, or ever again having to live "under the circumstances." In Philippians 4:8,9, Paul admonished the Christians in Philippi to focus their attention on truth:

> *"Finally, brethren, whatever is true, whatever is honorable, whatever is right, whatever is pure, whatever is lovely, what ever is of good repute, if there is any excellence and if anything worthy of praise, let your mind dwell on these things. The things you have learned and received and heard and seen in me, practice these things; and the God of peace shall be with you."*

Identifying the false beliefs is the first step on our path toward new freedom in Jesus Christ. Once we recognize that many of our deeply held beliefs are actually rooted in deception, we can proceed to use our emotions as a checkpoint to determine if our beliefs about a given circumstance are based on truth or lies. Most of our painful emotions, such as fear, anger, and tension, are the product of believing Satan's lies. Therefore, when we have those emotions, we can ask ourselves, "What am I believing in this situation?" In almost every case, we will be able to trace the negative emotions back to one of the four false beliefs we have examined. Then we can choose to reject the lie we have identified and replace it with the corresponding truth from the Scriptures. This process is amazingly simple, yet amazingly profound and applicable. Here is an example:

Scott was working hard in the office on a mortgage loan proposal when his boss walked in to check on his progress. James, another man in the office who wanted a promotion very badly, made a joke about all the papers scattered on Scott's desk. Their boss had a good laugh, and they walked out together. Scott was furious! He had worked diligently on that proposal, and it was excellent, yet James had made fun of him in front of his boss. But instead of fuming about the incident all day, Scott used his anger as a gauge for his beliefs. He stopped and asked himself, "Why am I responding this way? What am I believing?" That was easy. He identified the false belief, "*I must be approved by certain others to feel good about myself.*" Scott acknowledged that the belief was a lie, rejected it, and affirmed the truth that he was totally accepted by God, and that God's acceptance is far more important than his boss' acceptance. Instead of wasting the day stewing in his anger, he was able to relax and glorify God by his attitude.

In examining our emotions, it is important to realize that not all distressing emotions reflect deception. For example, the emotion of remorse might be the conviction of the Holy Spirit leading us to repentance. Not all anger and fear are wrong. Anger at someone molesting a child or beating an elderly person is a righteous anger, just as a measure of fear while driving during rush hour in Houston is entirely justifiable! The Christian who regularly replaces his false beliefs with God's truths will be equipped to discern between emotions that are the product of a righteous response and those that are the product of Satan's deceptions.

In our problem-filled world, there are two ways, both erroneous, that most people choose to deal with their emotions and the circumstances surrounding them. One way that people deal with emotions is to shut them out completely, refusing to acknowledge them or be affected by them. However, switching off our emotions in this way can cause us to become callous and insensitive to ourselves and others around us. Unfortunately, this is just what happened to Mike. Over the years, Mike had deadened himself to his emotions, apparently not allowing anything to bother him. He had experienced a difficult childhood, first being abandoned by his parents, and then being shuffled from one relative to another. In an effort to stop the pain, Mike learned to block out his emotions and to ignore his circumstances.

But Mike's success at suppressing his emotions had long-lasting consequences. First, by severing himself from the painful emotions, he missed out on many pleasant emotions as well. Secondly, the longer Mike avoided dealing with his emotions, the more fearful he became of them. To combat this fear, he simply became more calloused and withdrawn. Third, and perhaps most important, Mike could not use his emotions to detect the false beliefs that were at the root of his problem because he denied that he even had those emotions. He was helpless, unable to acknowledge his needs.

The second way that many people deal with emotions is by becoming enslaved to their emotions, unable or unwilling to make decisions that are contrary to them. Wearing her emotions on her sleeve, Melinda was not difficult to figure out. Her flaring temper, her torrent of tears, and her jovial laughter were all indications of her rollercoaster emotions. Never knowing what to expect, Melinda's husband, Ken, became weary of trying to deal with his volatile wife.

Melinda's erratic emotions affected her so much that they became, in effect, her lord. Her feelings seemed to be more real than anything else in her life and clouded her perception of God and His purposes.

We often respond incorrectly to them, but our emotions are in fact a gift from God, intended to be used and enjoyed. In His goodness, God intended us to live in joy and peace, buoyed by love, and anchored by faith, but until His truth is dominant in our lives, our emotions will determine our responses to life's situations.

It is vital that we be sensitive to our emotions and actions, always looking for those that do not reflect the character of our Lord Jesus Christ. We need to submit these painful emotions and actions to Him in prayer, asking that He reveal the false beliefs that hinder our fellowship with Him. Then empowered by the Holy Spirit, we can cast aside our false beliefs and choose to believe the truths of God's Word. (The Psalmist modeled the freedom to express both joy and pain to God. For example, look at Psalms 6 and 13.) Notice, it is first necessary to expose the root emotions and the false beliefs which are triggering them. Then secondly, by faith, we can allow God's Word to renew our minds.

Here are ten typical statements reflecting common false beliefs. Examine each statement, asking, "What false belief(s) does this statement represent?" Then beside each statement, place the number of one or more of the false beliefs. All ten statements are reflections of the four false beliefs we hve already studied:

(1)   *I must meet certain standards to feel good about myself;*
(2)   *I must be approved by certain others to feel good about myself;*
(3)   *Those who fail are unworthy of love and deserve to be blamed and condemned;*
(4)   *I am what I am; I cannot change; I am hopeless.*

1.   Tammy is right. I'll never be a successful husband and father.
2.   I'm so undisciplined. I'll never be able to accomplish anything.
3.   I just can't trust God.
4.   My father never did accept me.
5.   That's just the way I am.
6.   Everything I do turns out badly.
7.   I failed my college final. I'll never graduate now.
8.   I can't overcome a particular sin.
9.   I am going to fail financially.
10.   I deserve all the misery I am experiencing.

Compare your answers with these:

1.	1,4	6.	1
2.	1,4	7.	1,3
3.	4	8.	4
4.	2	9.	1
5.	4	10.	3

Were you able to identify the false beliefs? If not, look at the statements again carefully, analyzing the root issue behind each one.

One of the main reasons we tend to respond poorly to circumstances is that we think we deserve better. Our society and media tell us that everybody should be happy, comfortable, healthy, and successful. The difficulty arises when we believe these statements and equate orthodox Christianity with a comfortable middle-class life-style. We think we deserve the best of everything, so when things don't go the way we'd like, we get upset.

What do you think you deserve? Do you think you deserve appreciation from your friends, success in school or in your career, a clear complexion, good health, a promotion, leisure time, or freedom from whining children, an insensitive spouse, or inconsiderate neighbors? We sometimes are unable to identify the particular status or comfort we think we deserve, but we are sure we deserve better than what we're experiencing. One of the most obvious results of this perspective is a lack of thankfulness and contentment.

There are three principles from the Scriptures that can significantly help us understand what we deserve:

1. *The transcendent purposes of God.*

The prophet Isaiah wrote that God's wisdom and purposes far surpass our own:

> *"For My thoughts are not your thoughts, Neither are your ways My ways, declares the Lord. For as the heavens are higher than the earth, So are My ways higher than your ways, And My thoughts than your thoughts" (Isaiah 55:8, 9).*

One of the reasons we think we deserve better is that we believe we know what is best for us and for others. But are we omniscient? Are we sovereign, gracious and good like God? That is the issue, isn't it? Do we deserve better than the sovereign purposes of the Almighty God?

2. *A humble view of ourselves.*

Christ told a parable to explain our proper relationship to God:

> *"But which of you, having a slave plowing or tending sheep, will say to him when he has 'Come in from the field, come immediately and sit down to eat'?*
>
> *"But will he not say to him, 'Prepare something for me to eat, and properly clothe yourself and serve me until I have eaten and drunk; and afterward you will eat and drink'?*
>
> *"He does not thank the slave because he did the things which were commanded, does he?*
>
> *"'So you too, when you do all the things which are commanded you, say, 'We are unworthy slaves; we have done only that which we ought to have done'"* *(Luke 17:7-10).*

He is the Lord. He is the One who rightly deserves our affection and joyful obedience. Jesus said of the servant in this passage, if he did all that he was commanded, he was still to think of himself as an unworthy servant. "Unworthy? I thought we were deeply loved and accepted by God." This passage does not contradict the Biblical truths we have examined. It is teaching a different issue than the basis of acceptance before God: that He is the sovereign Lord and He does not owe us anything. All that we have is by His grace. We are the thankful recipients, and He is the gracious and loving Lord.

The problem appears when we do something "for the Lord": Bible study, church attendance, witnessing, being kind to someone, etc., and we think that He is then obligated to bless us. God is never obligated to bless us, but He does what is best for His honor and our growth.

3. *Overwhelming thankfulness for our forgiveness.*

In Luke 7:36-50, a woman who is overcome with thankfulness for her forgiveness is contrasted with a Pharisee who is not thankful:

> *"Now one of the Pharisees was requesting Him to dine with him. And He entered the Pharisee's house, and reclined at the table. And behold, there was a woman in the city who was a sinner; and when she learned that He was reclining at*

the table in the Pharisee's house, she brought an alabaster vial of perfume, and standing behind Him at His feet, weeping, she began to wet His feet with her tears, and kept wiping them with the hair of her head, and kissing His feet, and anointing them with the perfume.

"Now when the Pharisee who had invited Him saw this, he said to himself, If this man were a prophet He would know who and what sort of person this woman is who is touching Him, that she is a sinner.'

"And Jesus answered and said to him, 'Simon, I have something to say to you.' And he replied, 'Say it, Teacher.'

"A certain moneylender had two debtors: one owed five hundred denarii, and the other fifty. When they were unable to repay, he graciously forgave them both. Which of them therefore will love him more?'

"Simon answered and said, 'I suppose the one whom he forgave more.' And He said to him, 'You have judged correctly.' And turning toward the woman, He said to Simon, 'Do you see this woman? I entered your house; you gave Me no water for My feet, but she has wet My feet with her tears, and wiped them with her hair, you gave Me no kiss; but she, since the time I came in, has not ceased to kiss My feet, you did not anoint My head with oil, but she anointed My feet with perfume, for this reason I say to you, her sins, which are many, have been forgiven, for she loved much; but he who is forgiven little, loves little, And He said to her, 'Your sins have been forgiven.'

"And those who were reclining at the table with Him began to say to themselves, who is this man who even forgives sins?' And He said to the woman, 'Your faith has saved you; go in peace.'"

Is your response to Christ more like the Pharisee or more like the woman? When we grasp even a portion of the magnitude of

Christ's love and forgiveness, we will overflow with appreciation to Him.

After all, what we really deserve is the righteous condemnation of God. Our rebellion deserves the punishment of hell, but we have been spared that because Christ experienced God's wrath for us on the cross. It is very instructive if we realize this: Anything that happens to us that is better than hell is by the grace of God. That should help us get out of the mire of self-pity, and instead experience contentment, thankfulness, and the joy of Christ!

What upsets you? What do you think you deserve? Learn to focus on what you have that you don't deserve instead of what you don't have that you think you deserve. That realization will have a radical impact on your outlook on life.

Chapter Eleven

The Weapons of our Warfare

One of the biggest steps toward consistently glorifying Christ, bearing His image, and walking in peace and joy with our Heavenly Father is recognizing the deceit which has held us captive. Satan's four basic lies have distorted our true perspective, warped our thoughts, and tormented our emotions. If we cannot identify those lies, then it is very likely that we will continue to be defeated by them.

However, simply realizing the source of our problems will not set us free from them. Once we recognize the tricks of the enemy, we must seize the offense. We must use the weapons God has provided us to overcome incorrect thoughts, vain imaginations, and distorted beliefs. Paul describes the Christian's armor and weapons this way:

> *"Therefore, take up the full armor of God, that you may*
> *be able to resist in the evil day, and having done everything,*
> *to stand firm. Stand firm therefore, having girded your loins*
> *with truth, and having put on the breastplate of righteous-*
> *ness, and having shod your feet with the preparation of the*
> *gospel of peace; in addition to all, taking up the shield of*

faith with which you will be able to extinguish all the flaming missiles of the evil one. And take the helmet of salvation, and the sword of the Spirit, which is the word of God" (Ephesians 6:13-17).

Paul instructs us to put on the full armor of God. This armor is a defensive weapon, able to protect us from the attacks of Satan. Paul goes on to encourage us to take up the *"sword of the Spirit, which is the word of God."* In contrast to the defensive armor, this weapon, the Word of God, is an offensive weapon and is used to attack the enemy and conquer him. Paul indicates Christ did not intend for Christians to sit idly in their armor and absorb attack after attack from Satan. Instead, the wise warrior will reach for his offensive weapon and destroy the fortresses of the enemy. Applying this to our study, we need to take the truths of God's Word and use them to attack and overcome the lies of Satan.

Paul explains the nature of our warfare:

"For though we walk in the flesh, we do not war according to the flesh, for the weapons of our warfare are not of the flesh, but divinely powerful for the destruction of fortresses. We are destroying speculations and every lofty thing raised up against the knowledge of God, and we are taking every thought captive to the obedience of Christ" (II Corinthians 10:3-5).

These fortresses are belief systems based on Satan's lies. They are overcome by *"destroying speculations and every lofty thing raised up against the knowledge of God,"* that is, identifying and rejecting specific lies, then replacing them with the truth.

In the same letter to the Christians in Corinth, Paul shows how repentance can be a vital weapon in our warfare. If we have been deceived by the enemy, or if we have been involved in willful disobedience to God, we can repent by turning from our sin to God. Paul rejoiced that the Corinthians repented and experienced the grace of God:

> "I now rejoice, not that you were made sorrowful, but that you were made sorrowful to the point of repentance; for you were made sorrowful according to the will of God, in order that you might not suffer loss in anything through us. For the sorrow that is according to the will of God produces a repentance without regret, leading to salvation; but the sorrow of the world produces death" (II Corinthians 7:9, 10).

The Corinthians' example demonstrates repentance as a tactical weapon of our spiritual warfare. Repentance means to change, to change one's mind, purpose, and actions. It is more than just sorrow; it is the changing of our attitude and actions when we have realized that an attitude or an action is sinful and dishonoring to God.

As an offensive weapon, repentance possesses two sharp edges. The first edge of repentance allows us to discern and reject false beliefs. When situations occur which trigger certain beliefs that produce ungodly responses, we must:

1. recognize our emotion;
2. trace the emotion back to its source and identify the false belief; then,
3. consciously and assertively reject this false belief.

The following diagram illustrates this:

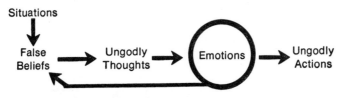

Trace the emotions back to the false beliefs

The second edge of repentance is the replacement of false beliefs with the truth of God's Word. By affirming God's truth about our worth, we will lodge this truth deep into our hearts and minds and begin to reshape our thinking. Then, the truth will set us free!

If false beliefs remain in our minds unchallenged and un-rejected, they retain an unconscious influence on our emotions and reactions. Consequently, our warfare is a sustained and continuous battle. Every disturbing situation provides us an opportunity to discover our incorrect thinking, to reject our world-acquired beliefs, and exchange them for truth. This is a daily process for every Christian; only this aggressive, conscious, truth-seeking effort can reverse years of habitually wrong thinking.

Affirming God's truth is a weapon of great spiritual value. Through this process, we state God's truth as our own perspective. Continual affirmation produces beliefs which result in correct thinking, which then result in godly responses. Affirming the truths of God's Word enables us to overcome the deception of the enemy (Revelation 12:10). The following diagram illustrates this process:

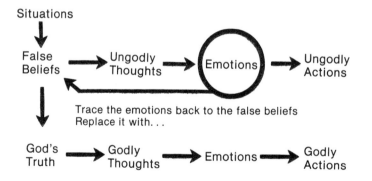

To effectively utilize affirmation as a weapon for change, remember these five concepts:

First, affirming the truths of the Scriptures does not mean the natural mind is in agreement with what we are affirming. The Bible teaches that the natural mind is antagonistic toward God:

"But a natural man does not accept the things of the Spirit of God; for they are foolishness to him, and he cannot understand them, because they are spiritually appraised" (I Corinthians 2:14).

It may not be comfortable to reflect on the truths of God's Word because the truths of the Spirit and the lies of the enemy are in opposition to one another. Therefore, don't be surprised by spiritual conflict when you confront these lies with God's truths.

Second, realize that these changes do not take place in our lives simply by a self-improvement program. The Holy Spirit is our Helper, and He will point out instances when we are believing Satan's lies; He will give insight into the truth of the Scriptures; and He will give strength to persevere in the spiritual battle. Even our desire to honor Christ is the work of the Holy Spirit in our lives. Through His wisdom and power, and our moment by moment choice to follow Him, the Holy Spirit produces changes in our lives for the glory of Christ.

Third, to become proficient at affirming these truths, we need to become students of God's Word and allow its truth to lodge deep within our hearts and minds. We should make it a regular practice to meditate upon the Word of God so that He can use it to change our beliefs, thoughts, emotions, and actions. David explained the power of applying the Scriptures:

"Thy Word I have treasured in my heart that I may not sin against thee.... "If Thy law had not been my delight, then I would have perished in my affliction. I will never forget Thy precepts, for by them Thou hast revived me.... "Thy word is a

> *lamp to my feet, and a light to my path....* "*Therefore I love*
> *Thy commandments above gold, yes, above fine gold*"
> *(Psalm 119: 11,92-93,105,127).*

Fourth, affirm the truth that specifically corresponds to a particular false belief. Once we have identified a specific false belief as the cause of our improper emotional or behavioral reaction, we should claim God's corresponding truth in the situation. (See the chart at the end of Chapter 8.)

Finally, take time to reflect on the marvelous Biblical truth outlined in this book. It is not the unthinking, mechanical utterance of these truths which produces freedom, but the conscious realization of the truth which changes our minds and actions. For example, when we affirm that we are deeply loved by God, we should think through the doctrine of propitiation, if possible, quoting I John 4:9,10 audibly. The power of God's Word will conquer the false belief and liberate our minds.

Let me illustrate how applying the truth affected a young woman I counselled. Peggy had given up any hope that her life could ever have any true value. She held to the false belief that she would be what she had always been: a failure.

"That's just me. I can't do any better than this," she would always tell herself. But once Peggy began to affirm her self-worth in God's eyes, she began correcting her false beliefs.

"No, that's not me," she began to say to herself. "On the contrary, *I am loved, forgiven, accepted, and complete in Jesus Christ.* That's the real me!"

In a short time, Peggy found herself believing the truth, and eventually her emotions and behavior reflected those truths.

In much the same way, a young man named Carl began to understand the cause of his depression, and he began to counter it by reflecting on God's truth about himself. "I have believed that *I must meet certain standards in order to feel good about myself,*" he reasoned.

"I have believed that I'm a failure and cannot meet these standards. However, this isn't true. I have failed in my performance, but poor performance isn't the real me. It's only a reflection of the deception I have been believing. Instead of accepting my poor past performance as the basis of my self-worth, I choose to believe *I am completely forgiven and fully pleasing to God.*" Then he meditated on Romans 5:1:

> *"Therefore, having been justified by faith, we have peace with God through our Lord Jesus Christ."*

Carl reflected, "I choose to believe the truth of God's Word instead of my own perception of myself. I choose to believe *I am deeply loved by God.*" He thought about the truth of I John 4:9,10:

> *"By this the love of God was manifested in us, that God has sent His only begotten Son into the world so that we might live through Him. In this is love, not that we loved God, but that He loved us and sent His Son to be the propitiation for our sins."*

The weapon of repentance, through rejection of false beliefs and affirmation of godly truth, has changed thousands of lives. As we saw in the cases of Peggy and Carl, it can liberate the mind and *"destroy speculations and every lofty thing raised up against the knowledge of God"* (I Cor. 10:5). And it can help us discover the wondrous significance we have in Jesus Christ: *We are deeply loved, completely forgiven, fully pleasing, totally acceptable and complete in Christ.* Our journey is a joyous and challenging adventure with Christ.

Now that we understand the value of the weapon of repentance, we will look further to the subjects of guilt, conviction, affirmation, and faith.

Chapter Twelve

Guilt vs. Conviction

There is a truth in God's Word that allows me to say without reservation that there is no reason whatsoever for a Christian to experience the gnawing pain of guilt. What insight permits me to make such an unqualified statement? My liberty stems from the reality of New Testament truth: not once does the New Testament speak of Christians as worthy of condemnation.

In Romans 8:1, Paul points out, *"There is therefore now no condemnation for those who are in Christ Jesus."* So, how can I say that no Christian need experience guilt? Because Paul said it first!

When I shared this important truth with a troubled Christian brother, I watched his jaw drop and tears fill his eyes. He looked at me incredulously and exclaimed, "You mean all this guilt I have been carrying for so long is unnecessary? You mean I can be free from this sense of condemnation and torment? Why hasn't somebody told me this before?"

The apostle Paul has been trying to tell us just that for centuries, but few Christians have listened. We feel we deserve condemnation, and we fail to realize that Christ has set us free from the guilt and condemnation for our sins.

What exactly is guilt, anyway? Sigmund Freud said that guilt is a result of social restraint. To Freud, guilt was born in the mind of a child when his parents scolded him and was nothing more than the fear of losing the love of someone significant to him. Therefore, according to Freud, guilt comes when we fear a loss of social esteem, when instinctive drives cause us to act in ways other than the accepted social norm.

Alfred Adler wrote that guilt arises from a refusal to accept one's inferiority. Therefore, he said, guilt feelings are those pangs of self-incrimination we feel anytime we think or behave inadequately. Both Freud and Adler tried to explain the pain of guilt from a perspective that denies the righteous judgment of God and our personal responsibility for sin. To them, guilt could only be explained on a human, existential basis.

Christian authors, Bruce Narramore and Bill Counts, represent a more Biblical perspective when they differentiate between true guilt and false guilt. True guilt, they explain, is an objective fact, but false guilt is a subjective feeling of pain and rejection. They emphasize that while the Bible discusses the fact of legal or theological guilt, it never tells the Christian to feel psychological guilt. These distinctions are helpful, but they may not clarify the issue for those people who equate *any* guilt with condemnation. For this reason, it is better to use the terms "guilt" and "conviction" to distinguish between the condemnation deserved for sin and the loving prodding of God to live in a way that honors Him. Though many people confuse these two, they are actually worlds apart. The chart later in this chapter clearly illustrates the differences.

No emotion is more destructive than guilt. It causes a loss of self-respect. It causes the human spirit to wither, and eats away at our personal significance. Guilt is a strong motivation, but it plays on a person's fear of failure and rejection; therefore, it can never ultimately build, encourage, or inspire us in our desire to live for Christ.

Some people understand guilt as a sense of legal and moral accountability before God. They distinguish it from low self-esteem by reasoning that guilt is the result of a sinful act or moral wrongdoing, while low self-esteem is derived from a feeling of social or personal inadequacy. Consequently, a lie makes us feel unacceptable to God and brings guilt, while bad table manners make us feel unacceptable to the people around us and bring low self-esteem.

This perspective shows some depth of thought, but it focuses on the emotional response rather than the root cause. At its root, guilt is the condition of being separated from God and deserving condemnation for sin. Low self-esteem can be experienced by Christians or non-Christians, anyone who believes Satan's lies and feels like a failure: hopeless and rejected.

As we have determined, guilt has a restricted meaning in the New Testament. It refers only to man's condition prior to his salvation. Only the non-Christian is guilty before God. He has transgressed the law of God and must face the consequences. Guilt shakes its fist and says, "You have fallen short and must pay the price. You are personally accountable." Only in Christ is our condemnation removed. Christ removed our guilt when He accepted the penalty for our sins. He died on the cross with the burden of our guilt, suffering the full punishment for all sin. Because of His substitution, we need never face guilt's consequences. We are acquitted and absolved from our guilt, free from our sentence of spiritual death.

Many of us have been told that we are still guilty even after we have trusted Christ to pay for our sins. And sadly, we have heard this in churches, places that should be loudly and clearly proclaiming the forgiveness, freedom, and zeal found in the cross. Learn to identify incorrect teaching, guilt motivation, and the pang of guilt in your own thoughts. Then refuse to believe the lies any longer, and focus on the unconditional love and acceptance of Christ. Perhaps some people think that if they don't use guilt motivation, people won't do anything. That may be true for a short while until the people adjust to being motivated properly, but that short period of waiting is well worth the long-term results of grace-oriented intrinsic motivation. The love of Christ is powerful, and He is worthy of our intense zeal to obey and honor Him. The result of proper motivation is an enduring, deepening commitment to Christ and His cause, rather than the prevalent results of guilt motivation: resentment and the desire to escape.

Although Christians are free from guilt, we are still subject to the conviction of sin. The Bible frequently speaks of the Holy Spirit's work to convict believers of sin. He directs and encourages our spiritual progress by revealing our sins in contrast to the holiness and purity of Christ.

Although the Holy Spirit convicts both believers and unbelievers of sin (John 16:8), His conviction of believers is not intended to produce the pangs of guilt. Our status and self-worth are secure by the grace of God, and we are no longer guilty. Conviction deals with our behavior, not our status before God. Conviction is the Holy Spirit's way of showing the error of our performance in light of God's standard and truth. His motivation is love, correction, and protection.

While guilt is applicable to non-believers and originates from Satan, conviction is the privilege of those who believe and is given by the Holy Spirit. Guilt brings depression and despair, but conviction leads us to the beautiful realization of God's forgiveness and the experience of His love and power.

Perhaps the following summary will better reveal the contrasting purposes and results of guilt and conviction:

Basic Focus:

GUILT focuses on the state of being condemned: *"I am unworthy."*

CONVICTION focuses on behavior: *"This act is unworthy of Christ and is destructive."*

Primary Concern:

GUILT deals with the sinner's loss of self-esteem and a wounded self-pride: *"What will others think of me?"* CONVICTION deals with the loss of our moment by moment communion with God: *"This act is destructive to me and interferes with my walk with God."*

Primary Fear:

GUILT produces a fear of punishment: *"Now I'm going to get it!"* CONVICTION produces a fear of the destructiveness of the act itself: *"This behavior is destructive to me and others, and it robs me of what God intends for me."*

Agent:

The agent of GUILT is Satan: *"... the god of this world has blinded the minds of the unbelieving, that they might not see the light of the gospel of the glory of Christ"* (II Corinthians 4:4). The agent of CONVICTION is the Holy Spirit: *". . . but if by the Spirit you are putting to death the deeds of the body, you will live"* (Romans 8:13).

Behavioral Results:

GUILT leads to depression and more sin: *"I am just a low-down, dirty, rotten sinner;* or to rebellion: *"I don't care. I'm going to do whatever I want to do."* CONVICTION leads to repentance, the turning from sin to Christ: *"Lord, I agree with You that my sin is wrong and destructive. What do You want me to do?"*

Interpersonal Result:

The interpersonal result of GUILT is alienation, a feeling of shame that drives one away from the person who has been wronged: *"I can't ever face him again."*

The interpersonal result of CONVICTION is restoration, a desire to remedy the harm done to others: *"Father, what would You have me do to right this wrong and restore the relationship with those I have offended?"*

Distinguishing After-Effects:

GUILT ends in depression, bitterness and self-pity: *"I'm just no good."*
CONVICTION ends in comfort, the realization of forgiveness: *"Thank You, Lord, that I am completely forgiven and totally accepted by you!"*

Remedy:

The remedy for GUILT is to trust in Christ's substitutionary death to pay for the condemnation for sin.
The remedy for CONVICTION is confession, agreeing with God that our sin is wrong, that Christ has forgiven us, and that our attitude and actions will change.

Although Christians are no longer subject to condemnation, we will not be free from its destructive power until we learn to distinguish between guilt and conviction. The Holy Spirit wants us to be convinced that we are forgiven, accepted, and loved -- totally secure because of Christ. The Holy Spirit is the "paraclete," or one "called along side," to lift us up and encourage us. As a part of His ministry, He faithfully makes us aware of any behavior that does not reflect the characteristics of Christ. He helps us understand both our righteousness before God and the failures in our performance.

What can we conclude from these truths? We can conclude that guilt is rooted in condemnation, but conviction leads us to confession and repentance and to a renewed realization of God's grace and forgiveness.

Knowing this, how can we deal with feelings of guilt? First, we need to affirm that Christ has forgiven us and made us judicially righteous. Our sin does not bring condemnation, but it is harmful and dishonors God. We can confess our sin to God, claim the forgiveness we already have in Christ, and then move on in joy and freedom to honor Him. The following prayer expresses this attitude:

"Father, I affirm that I am deeply loved by you, that I am fully pleasing to You, and I am totally accepted in Your sight. You have made me complete and given me the righteousness of Christ, even though my performance often falls short.

"Lord, I confess my sins to You. (List them. Be specific.) I agree with You that these are wrong. Thank You for Your grace and forgiveness. Is there anything I need to return, anyone I need to repay, or anyone I need to apologize to? Thank You."

It is important to affirm our righteousness in Christ as well as confess our sins. God does not need to be reminded of our right standing in Him, but we do. Therefore, we need to make this prayer a daily experience and let it pervade our thoughts and hearts. As we yield to the gentle prodding of God-given conviction, confess our sins, and affirm our true relationship with Him, we are gradually shaped and molded so that we may increasingly honor *"the One who died and rose again on our behalf"* *(II Cor. 5:15).*

Chapter Thirteen

The Search Concluded

As we conclude our examination of the search for significance, we will touch on several issues to help clarify how we apply the truths of the Scriptures. We will look at: the contrast between our old and new natures; how we can honor Christ; how faith operates; and finally, how to apply the concepts in this book. First, let's see how understanding the contrast between our old and new natures can help us grow in Christ and bring honor to Him.

Living freely and fully in Christ requires that we constantly be on the alert against our former ways of thinking, and actively choose the qualities of Christ over the enticing deception of the world. Time after time, Scripture instructs us to exercise our wills to free us from our old way of living. As Paul taught the believers in Ephesus:

"...In reference to your former manner of life, you lay aside the old self, which is being corrupted in accordance with the lusts of deceit, and that you be renewed in the spirit of your mind, and put on the new self, which in the likeness

of God has been created in righteousness and holiness of the truth" (Ephesian 4:22-24).

In this passage, Paul explains that Christians have two natures which he calls "the old self" and "the new self." What exactly is the old self that must be laid aside? The old self is the sinful, fallen nature we possess as descendants of Adam. We know from Scripture that the old self is corrupted by the lusts of deceit (Ephesians 4:22), is involved in evil practices such as lying, slander, abusive speech, idolatry, wrath, malice, immorality, impurity, passion, evil desire and greed (Colossians 3:8, 9), and is a body of sin (Romans 6:6).

In contrast, the new self is the nature given to us by God when we trust Christ as our Savior. This nature bears the characteristics of Christ. It has been created *"in the likeness of God in righteousness and holiness" (Ephesians 4:24),* and is strengthened according to God's power (Ephesians 3:16). The new self is a reality for all individuals born of the Spirit.

As we know, man lost his ability to reflect the image of God after the Fall. Now, through faith in Jesus Christ, we are released from the domination of the natural man and able to put on the new self and bear His image. Although we are free from sin's absolute domination, we are not free from the influence of the old nature. Until we die and leave our physical bodies behind and live with Christ, the new self will continually war against the old self. Our spiritual desires will battle our lustful, worldly desires and the natural mind will clash with the truths of the Scriptures (Galatians 5:16-24).

Unless we are diligent, we can grow weary of this spiritual warfare, and succumb to the lusts and pride in which the world delights. When we acquiesce, we adopt our old emotions and habits again. Giving in may seem attractive at the time, but it leads to feelings of failure and low self-esteem, and it dishonors the Lord. Clearly, momentary escape from the battle isn't worth it. It only appears to be escape; actually it is exchanging one battle with the Lord as our powerful ally, for another battle with the Lord as our loving adversary who wants to correct our error.

The more we understand Biblical truth about ourselves, the better we will be able to wage spiritual warfare. The apostle Paul clearly distinguished between the character and results of the old self and the new self. His delineation in Romans 6 centers on four words: know, consider, present, and obey. Let's examine these.

In Romans 6:3-10, Paul instructs us to know the basic facts about who we are in Christ:

> *"Or do you not know that all of us who have been baptized into Christ Jesus have been baptized into His death? Therefore we have been buried with Him through baptism into death, in order that as Christ was raised from the dead through the glory of the Father, so we too might walk in newness of life. For if we have become united with Him in the likeness of His death, certainly we shall be also in the likeness of His resurrection, Knowing this, that our old self was crucified with Him, that our body of sin might be done away with, that we should no longer be slaves to sin; For he who has died is freed from sin.*
>
> *"Now if we have died with Christ, we believe that we shall also live with Him, knowing that Christ, having been raised from the dead, is never to die again: death no longer is master over Him. For the death that He died, He died to sin, once for all" (Romans 6:3-10).*

Our old self, which deserved the condemnation of God, was identified with Christ on the cross. Our old self was crucified with Him, the penalty for sin was fully paid by Christ, and we now live, identified with Christ's resurrection *"so we too might walk in newness of life."* Paul wants us to be well aware of these facts so that we can draw definite conclusions from them.

Verse 11 tells us to reflect on and consider the facts already presented:

> "*Even so consider yourselves to be dead to sin, but alive to God in Christ Jesus*" (Romans 6:11).

To "consider" means to be deeply convinced of truth so that we rely on it. Unless we take the time to reflect on the implications of our identity with Christ in His death and resurrection, these most important events in history will be like facts learned in a history class about some war fought long ago. We may be able to recite the dates, names, and places, but those facts won't make any difference in our lives. The magnificent truths of our identity in Christ deserve far more attention than our ability to parrot back the facts. They deserve deep reflection on their implications in our relationships, goals, and self-esteem.

If we understand the implications of Christ's death and resurrection, that our old self died with Christ and our new self came to life in Him, then our logical, heart-felt response will be to present ourselves to Him:

> "*Therefore do not let sin reign in your mortal body that you should obey its lusts, And do not go on presenting the members of your body to sin as instruments of unrighteousness; but present yourselves to God as those alive from the dead, and your members as instruments of righteousness to God*" (Romans 6:12-13).

We have a choice, to present the members of our bodies (our thoughts; wills, goals, desires, and actions) either to sin or to God. One results in more unrighteous behavior, it is harmful to us and others, and it dishonors God. The other results in righteous behavior, enables us to grow and serve, and brings glory to God. The choice is clear, isn't it? Note that Paul doesn't start Romans 6 with the exhortation to present ourselves to God. The commitment to action follows understanding the facts and considering the implications of those facts. Then, the call to commitment seems reasonable, not forced. The Lord and the apostle Paul do not want us to commit ourselves to something we don't understand. Commitment must follow understanding or that commitment will be shallow and probably short-lived.

After presenting ourselves to God as a reasonable response to His grace, we then need to perpetuate that commitment through moment by moment obedience to Him:

> *"What then? Shall we sin because we are not under law but under grace? May it never be! Do you not know that when you present yourselves to someone as slaves for obedience, you are slaves of the one whom you obey, either of sin resulting in death, or of obedience resulting in righteousness? But thanks be to God that though you were slaves of sin, you became obedient from the heart to that form of teaching to which you were committed, And having been freed from sin, you became slaves of righteousness"* *(Romans 6:15-18).*

Paul indicates that it would be foolish for us to disobey because we have been freed from slavery to sin. It is right and proper to obey God because our new self in Christ is now our true source of identity. He uses the term "slaves" to signify obligation and mastery. Before we trusted Christ, we were slaves of sin, obligated to a lifestyle of unrighteousness, but now we are slaves of obedience to God, obligated to Christ, His teaching, and His righteousness.

As we identify our old selves as the fertile soil of Satan's deceptions, we will be more equipped to understand ourselves and deal properly with our ungodly thoughts, painful emotions, and unrighteous actions. Considering the old self to be dead does not mean that we deny that our distressing emotions exist. Indeed, they are very real, but we can now choose our response: to allow them to run rampant or to use them to identify false beliefs.

Following Christ can be difficult. Our culture suggests that the easy way is the right way, but in reality, neither way is easy. Following Christ is difficult because our culture, our old selves, and Satan fight against our desire to honor the Lord, but disobedience is difficult because of the pain and tragic consequences of sin. Some say that the world's way is easy; that is misleading. Others say that if you follow Christ, your life will be free from problems, but these well-meaning people are misleading, too. We will be much better off if we realize that there is no easy way to live. Comfort is not the goal. The goal, however difficult, is to honor Christ because He loves us and He is worthy of our faith, love, and obedience.

But what does it mean to honor Christ? What can we do to bring glory to Him? There are almost countless attitudes and activities that could be listed, but overall it means to accurately represent Him in every thought, action, relationship, and conversation -- to bear His image. The major categories of attitudes and activities that honor Christ include:

Love -- This love is unconditional affection for Christ, for other Christians, for unbelievers, and for ourselves. This love is not Pollyanna; it means that we care enough to correct as well as to encourage.

Holiness -- We generally think of holiness primarily in terms of what we don't do -- the abstinence from sin. But holiness also includes a positive side: zeal for Christ and His cause.

Biblical Values -- The more we understand the love and character of Christ, the more we will value the things that are important to Him. Prestige, money, success, and the approval of others will gradually lose their appeal, and instead, we will desire that Christ be honored, that people become Christians, that believers grow in their faith, and that missionaries are sent out to the world.

Giving --Jesus said to Nicodemus, *"For God so loved the world that He gave... " (John 3:16)*. The more we understand Him, the more we will be like Him. We have received so much from God in both the temporal and eternal realms, it is a joy to give to others in need. The measure of our lives should not be what we have, but how much we give.

Evangelism -- Christ has given us an example, a mission, and a command to reach others with the message of His love and forgiveness. The primary reason we don't tell more people is that we fear their rejection, but His acceptance of us transcends the disapproval of others. The world (and our neighbors) desperately needs to hear a clear, loving presentation of the gospel. It is our privilege as His chosen ambassadors to tell them.

Discipleship -- Christ discipled the people around Him by being a constant example as well as communicating truth. His example of love, humility, strength, and tenderness provided a powerful context for learning. If we want others to grow in their faith, we need to follow His example and model the life we study and teach.

Social Activism -- The influence of Christ should not be relegated only to the spiritual aspect of life. In the last century, William Wilburforce led the struggle against slavery in England, basing his arguments squarely on the Scriptures. In civil rights, politics, abortion, education, and every other area of life, Christ is the source of truth, justice, and love.

Prayer -- Christ said, *"Apart from Me, you can do nothing" (John 15:5).* How ridiculous it is (and in an eternal sense, unproductive) for us to be so busy with our programs and activities if they are not based on the Word of Christ and accomplished according to the power of Christ. Prayer is a reflection of our dependence on Him.

Worship -- Perhaps our greatest expression of love for God is worship -- speaking or singing of His greatness. Whether on Sunday morning with hundreds of others, or alone, worship properly reflects our dependence, thankfulness, and praise.

Glorifying God is not limited to any given time or place. It is our privilege at every moment to accurately reflect our Creator and Savior to others, to ourselves, or to Him. Why? Because He rightly deserves it. As the scene in heaven vividly depicts, Christ is worthy of our praise and obedience:

> *"And I looked, and I heard the voice of many angels around the throne and the living creatures and the elders; and the number of them was myriads of myriads, and thousands of thousands, Saying with a loud voice, 'Worthy is the Lamb that was slain to receive power and riches and wisdom and might and honor and glory and blessing'. And every created thing which is in heaven and on the earth and under the earth and on the sea, and all things in them, I heard saying, 'To Him who sits on the throne, and to the Lamb, be blessing and honor and glory and dominion forever and ever'. And the four living creatures kept saying, 'Amen'. And the elders fell down and worshiped"* (Revelation 5:11-14).

Throughout this book, we have also seen how sin plunged man into spiritual darkness and how that darkness has blinded our eyes to truth. We have seen how every individual born in sin has been deceived by false beliefs, resulting in improper thoughts, emotions, and actions. Through this veil of darkness, it is impossible for the sinful man to earn the love and acceptance of God.

But in this darkness, we have discovered a light as God Himself has provided a path to an intimate relationship with Him. That light is Jesus Christ, from whom we freely receive salvation, forgiveness, justification, propitiation, and acceptance. By faith, in a miraculous instant, we are adopted into a new family, we receive an inheritance as sons and daughters of God, and we are given the purpose of representing the Lord to those around us. The rest of our lives is spent in understanding and experiencing these incredible truths.

We have seen that our relationship with God, our security, and our self-worth are not earned by our efforts. They are obtained only by faith. This point is so important, let's take some time to analyze what faith is. Faith has several synonyms: trust, dependence, reliance, and belief. The focus is on the object of faith, not the faith itself. For example, if I believed a certain chair would hold me up if I sat in it, the primary issue would be the construction and quality of the chair --- the object of faith, not how much faith I have. Even if I believe very strongly that the chair will support me, if the chair is a rotten, broken-down piece of junk, then it will break if I try to sit in it. My faith will not make it a good chair. But if the chair is of quality construction, it only takes very little faith to sit comfortably in it. Again, it is the quality of the object, not the quantity of the faith, that is of primary importance.

In Christianity, Christ is the object of faith, and faith is our trust in the character and abilities of Christ. The more we know Him, the more we trust Him. Faith, then, requires our knowing God, and knowing Him requires a relationship. To know God, we need to talk to Him through prayer, listen to His voice, see Him at work in our lives and the lives of others, and search out His will and deeds through the Scriptures He has given us. *"So faith comes by hearing, and hearing by the word of Christ" (Romans 10:17).*

Make no mistake about it, faith is not a magic formula to manipulate God into granting us the wishes of our hearts. We cannot motivate God to act contrary to His sovereign will. Faith enables us to be partakers with Him, to gain wisdom from Him, and to bring His love and power to bear on human situations with lasting impact.

Let me explain it this way. Suppose Rusty needs $1,000 by Saturday to pay off an important obligation. Today is Wednesday, and Rusty has yet to raise the money. Rusty called John, a trusted friend. John was more than happy to supply the need, but he told Rusty to go home and wait until Saturday, the very day the money was due. "Give me until Saturday," John said. "I'll have the money for you by noon."

Rusty relaxed, realizing his need had been met. Although he had yet to actually see the money, he had confidence in his close friend. After all, John had always been reliable and he was a person of means. If he said he wanted to help meet Rusty's need and would supply the $1,000, certainly he would do so. Knowing that, Rusty could wait patiently until Saturday without anxiety. He had faith that John could and would deliver as promised because he had an intimate knowledge of John's proven character and ability.

Likewise, our faith in God rests just as surely in what we know of His character and ability. His character is love, revealed to us as a benevolent Father who desires to bestow good gifts to His children. And yet, a good Father knows that not all of the requests of His children are beneficial to them, and therefore some of them cannot be granted. We often find situations in life when we want something that seems very good and reasonable to us, but either God's Word opposes it or our prayers seem fruitless. There are three questions we need to ask in these situations:

Is it God's will? Do the Scriptures prohibit it, allow it, or promise it?

Is it for the glory of God? What is the motive - pleasure, prestige, or to honor Christ?

Is it His timing? Are there conditions to be met? Does He want me to wait?

It is then that we must exercise our faith to trust in His character alone even without visible evidence to support our trust. As the psalmist wrote:

> *"I would have despaired unless I had believed that I would see the goodness of the Lord in the land of the living. Wait for the Lord; be strong, and let your heart take courage; yes, wait for the Lord" (Psalm 27:13, 14).*

When we know Him and realize from His Word that He is both powerful and compassionate, we can then trust in Him despite what our feelings or human perceptions tell us.

Too often, however, we presume upon the will of God by rationalizing that what we are asking is beneficial to us. We think that God should be more than willing to grant our request; however, we must remember that God sees a bigger picture than we do. He can see the future, other relating circumstances, and all events that will affect our lives. Though we may ask a specific request according to His will, we must not despair if we do not see an immediate response. And we must remember that a creative God can take the best interests of all His children in interrelated events and resolve the matter in a way we least expect. The timing and methods of God are a mystery, and require our faith in His love and sovereignty:

> *"Oh, the depth of the riches both of the wisdom and knowledge of God! How unsearchable are His judgments and unfathomable His ways!" (Romans 11:33).*

The question is: Are we trusting the promises of God seeking them; or are we trusting the God of promise, seeking Him? This principle is evident in the case of Cathy. Cathy told me repeatedly that she just knew her husband David would come back to her. She had prayed for months that her family would be restored, and felt her prayer reflected the desire of God. Imagine how confused she looked when I asked her if God had told her that David would return home.

"Well, no, not exactly," she said, "but I really feel God wants us all together again, and I'm claiming it by faith."

It was good that Cathy was praying and waiting for David's return, but healing her home required that David obey God's voice and return of his own free will. When weeks went by and David didn't return, Cathy despaired. Was her faith misplaced? Was God unwilling to heal her home?

No, God was indeed willing to move on Cathy's behalf, but He would not violate David's free will. The choice remained with David, and Cathy would simply have to wait.

Cathy was frustrated, but she decided to study the sovereignty and wisdom of God. After a while, her frustration changed to faith and hope. Then, surprisingly, one day David came up the walk into the house. He was a changed man, and Cathy was a thrilled wife!

God answered Cathy's prayers by constructing circumstances that showed David his need for a Savior and for repentance, but it was David's decision to trust in Christ and come home. Our faith needs to be in God to do what the Scriptures say He will do, not to do things that violate His Word, His intentions, and the God-given free will of others.

There is another misunderstanding that needs to be dispelled. Some people believe that true faith exists only in the absence of doubt, but that is not necessarily the case. Biblical faith often exists in spite of our doubts. If we think that we need to be free from conflicting emotions and thoughts for our faith to be honoring to the Lord, we will be introspective and disappointed. Conflicting emotions and thoughts will be normal in our lives until we are set free from the old nature when we go to be with the Lord. Learn to be victorious in the conflict, not to deny its existence.

As an example of God-honoring faith in spite of doubts and conflicting emotions, look at the account of Abraham and Isaac. In Genesis 12:1-3 and Genesis 17:1-5, God established and repeated a solemn covenant with Abraham which included the promise to "*make you the father of a multitude of nations.*" (*Gen.17:5*) It probably didn't take Abraham long to figure out that if he was going to be the father of many nations, he would have to have at least one child! When he was 86 years old and Sarah, his wife, was 76 years old, Abraham had his first child, but there was a problem. This child was not Sarah's child. It was the child of Hagar, Sarah's maid. God indicated that the child, Ishmael, wasn't exactly what He had in mind as the first heir of the father of many nations. So after 14 long years, Abraham and Sarah (now 100 years old and 90 years old, respectively) miraculously had a son, Isaac. You can image how happy they were that God had given them this boy, the answer to His promise, when they were so far past the childbearing age!

But God was not through with Abraham. Genesis 22 records God's command to Abraham:

> *"Now it came about after these things, that God tested Abraham, and said to him, 'Abraham!' And he said, 'Here I am.' And He said, Take now your son, your only son, whom you love, Isaac, and go to the land of Moriah; and offer him there as a burnt offering on one of the mountains of which I will tell you" (Genesis 22:1,2).*

Do you think Abraham had some conflicting thoughts and emotions? The miracle-child, the first-born son, and heir to the promise of God to be offered as a burnt offering? We get a glimpse of the reasonings of Abraham's heart in the following verses:

> *"So Abraham rose early in the morning and saddled his donkey, and took two of his young men with him and Isaac his son; and he split wood for the burnt offering, and arose and went to the place of which God had told him. On the third day Abraham raised his eyes and saw the place from a distance. And Abraham said to his young men, 'Stay here with the donkey, and I and the lad will go yonder; and we will worship and return to you'" (Genesis 22:3-5).*

"We will worship and return to you," Abraham said. Hebrews 11:19 states that Abraham *"considered that God is able to raise men even from the dead."* Yes, Abraham would kill his only son if that is

what God required, but God surely will raise Isaac from the dead so that His promise would not be broken.

As it turned out, God stopped Abraham from killing Isaac, and Isaac did not have to be raised from the dead, but there is an important point for us to learn about dealing with conflicting thoughts and emotions: Act on the revealed will of God as explained in the Scriptures, and focus on the love, promises, and power of God. Abraham did not focus on his conflicting emotions or thoughts, though he probably had many of them. He didn't deny that he had them; he simply didn't let them determine his actions. The promise of God to provide an heir and the command of God to kill Isaac looked mutually exclusive, but the almighty, sovereign God is able to accomplish far more than we initially understand. We can have faith in His greatness, wisdom, and love, even when we don't understand what He is doing.

Christ, His Word, and His work to accomplish our redemption are worthy of our faith. At this point you may be asking, "How do I start applying these things?"

First, you need to understand the four truths of redemption and the corresponding four false beliefs that we mistake for truth. The ability to understand truth and recognize deception is a vital first step.

Secondly, learn to reject the lies and replace them with the Biblical truths so that your mind will be in the process of renewal. Along with renewing your mind, look for every opportunity to accurately and actively represent Christ in every situation and every relationship. The Search For Significance Workbook was developed to help you apply these truths so that your self-concept, your ambitions, and your relationships will begin to reflect the character of Christ.

Then third, teach these truths to others. Teaching is the best way to learn because you will pay closer attention and study more diligently if you are going to communicate them to someone else.

And fourth, endure. Develop a godly tenacity and keep following Christ. You will occasionally make mistakes, someone may disapprove of you, you may blame someone, you may occasionally fail to apply these truths, and you will occasionally dishonor the Lord, but realize that *you are deeply loved, completely forgiven and fully pleasing, totally accepted, and complete* because Christ died for you and was raised from the dead to give You new life. You are free! Free to *"proclaim the excellencies of Him who has called you out of darkness unto His marvelous light" (I Peter 2:9).*

*D*ear Friend,

In my heart, I feel that many people who read this book will be suffering from serious emotional or substance abuse problems or they will know someone who is. If so, I want them to know that there's hope.

You might be suffering yourself. And if you are, I want to assure you that there's hope for you, too, regardless of how serious your problems might be.

Our organization, RAPHA, provides Christ-centered treatment in hospitals and other settings where caring, committed professionals are seeing people of all ages healed of some of the most severe problems imaginable. The success stories we hear from children, youth and adults are indeed thrilling.

I want to encourage you to read the following pages very carefully. You will find information that will answer questions you might have about RAPHA and tell you more about the wide range of services we offer.

If you, personally, need help, or if you want to help someone, give us a call at 1-800-227-2657. Your inquiry will be strictly confidential.

Remember, we're here to serve you and to offer hope.

In Christ,

Robert S. McGee
President

"It has been good to know that we now have a place to refer persons we counsel who are in need of hospital care for emotional, spiritual and substance abuse problems."

Dr. Jerry Falwell
*Pastor, Thomas Road Baptist Church
Founder, Old-Time Gospel Hour
Chancellor, Liberty University
Lynchburg, Virginia*

"For years our churches have needed an anointed referral center to minister to those whose needs lie beyond the church counseling center. RAPHA is the answer."

Dr. Jimmy Draper
*Pastor, First Baptist Church
Euless, Texas
Past President of the Southern Baptist
Convention*

*"S*urely the ministry of RAPHA has been blessed by God! Christians everywhere should rejoice that there is such a program available in this country!"

T. W. Wilson
Associate to Billy Graham
Billy Graham Evangelistic Association

"I appreciate the commitment that RAPHA has for the American teenager. RAPHA's treatment program comes from a biblical perspective and has brought about true healing for emotional needs."

Dawson McAllister
President, Shepherd Productions
Irving, Texas

"RAPHA is an excellent balance of clinical and spiritual. They are treating needs in a unique and dynamic way."

Ben Kinchlow
Author/Speaker

"There has been a great need for treatment with a sound spiritual perspective. RAPHA offers that kind of program."

Pat Boone
Actor, Singer, Author and Chairman of the National Easter Seal Society

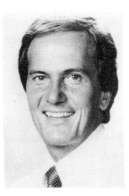

*"*R*APHA is committed to healing broken lives. I give it my heartiest endorsement and pray that God will use this ministry significantly."*

Dr. Lewis A. Drummond
President, Southeastern Baptist Theological Seminary
Wake Forest, North Carolina

*"*I *have longed for a Christ-centered ministry that addresses problems without sacrificing biblical principles. I believe* RAPHA *is such a program."*

Dr. Adrian Rogers
Pastor, Bellevue Baptist Church
Memphis, Tennessee
Past President of the Southern Baptist Convention

Christ-centered Hospital and Counseling Care

True stories of God's miracles through RAPHA

Depression

"After 21 years of depression and having been on several types of treatment units, I am at last finally free from depression. The RAPHA unit is a place where you can meet God face to face."

"I was about as far down as I could go. I thank RAPHA for its support, concern and patience. Thanks for lifting me up to higher ground!"

"I truly thank our wonderful Lord for RAPHA. I've been feeling just great! I have suddenly noticed the beautiful world around me and look up toward heaven to thank the Lord for the beautiful trees and grass and the singing birds. For so long--three years--while I was going through depression I never noticed the beauty around me! Isn't God great?"

RAPHA ministers to adults and adolescents.

Chemical Dependency

RAPHA has taught me so much. I'm not preaching to my friends that use drugs; I'm just being an example of how you can deal with your problems instead of using drugs as an escape."

"The RAPHA program is great! I'm doing so well and have had no trouble staying away from drugs."

"We want to express our appreciation to you for all the help you have given our family resulting in the admission of our son to your facility and for helping him to overcome his alcohol addiction."

Eating Disorders

"For over 17 years I had bulimia and was ready to take my life. If it were not for RAPHA, I would still have this terrible eating disorder. I'm a changed person; I'm a confident person with more self-esteem than I've ever had with a good positive attitude about life. I now realize that God loves me deeply, completely forgives me, that I'm fully pleasing to Him, totally acceptable to Him, and am complete in Christ. I like me. I now understand that I don't need to earn love, that I'm worthy to be loved, just as I am for who I am."

RAPHA provides general psychiatric and substance abuse treatment.

Other Disorders

- Suicidal and/or homicidal ideations or attempts
- Noticeable negative changes in behavior
- Poor impulse control (stealing, aggression, etc.)
- Violent outbursts toward others
- Progressive or extreme withdrawal
- Disordered, unmanageable behaviors
- Imminent failure of social, familial, or occupational functioning
- Mania

- Psychosis
- Paranoia, phobias
- Periods of confusion
- Severe loss of memory
- Delusional systems (hallucinations)
- Uncontrollably obsessive thoughts
- Anxiety attacks
- Multiple personality manifestations
- Impairment of thoughts, judgment, logic or reality testing
- Inability to carry out activities of daily living

Call RAPHA
Toll Free, 24 hours a day
1-800-227-2657

Confidentiality <u>is</u>
guaranteed.

What happens
when you
call RAPHA?

1. Evaluation will be made to determine if the person would benefit from one of RAPHA's programs.

2. The various treatment programs will be explained.

3. Financial aid and insurance availability will be explained.

4. If one of our programs is selected, admissions issues will be worked out prior to arrival at the treatment location. This includes travel aid, if needed.

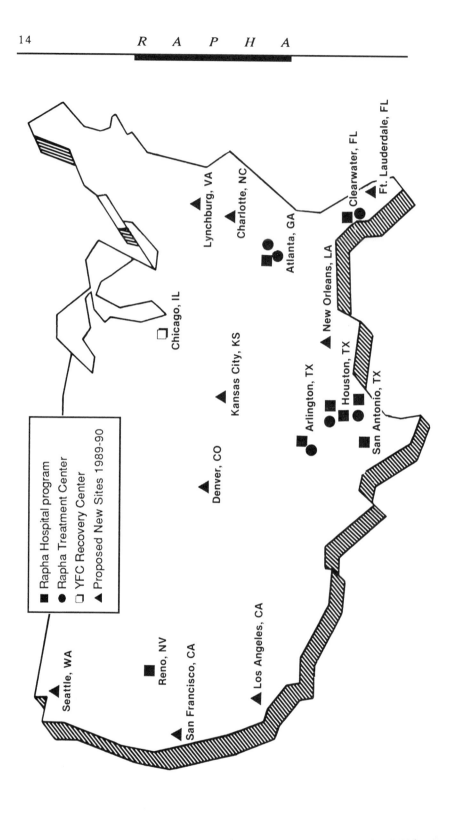

Rapha Hospital program

Rapha Treatment Center

YFC Recovery Center

Proposed New Sites 1989-90

Seattle, WA

Reno, NV

San Francisco, CA

Los Angeles, CA

San Antonio, TX

Denver, CO

Arlington, TX

Houston, TX

Kansas City, KS

Chicago, IL

New Orleans, LA

Lynchburg, VA

Charlotte, NC

Atlanta, GA

Clearwater, FL

Ft. Lauderdale, FL

What if you
live in another city?

In many cases, a Travel Assistance Program is available for air travel, ground transportation, escort personnel, and lodging, and will be carefully arranged for out-of-town patients who are unable to provide their own travel expenses to one of our hospitals or treatment centers listed below.

- HCA Deer Park Hospital
  Deer Park, Texas

- HCA Gulf Coast Hospital
  Baytown, Texas

- HCA Hill Country Hospital
  San Antonio, Texas

- Horizon Hospital
- Rapha Treatment Center--Fairwinds
  Clearwater, Florida

- HCA Houston International Hospital
- Rapha Treatment Center--Houston
- Rapha Treatment Center--Academy Hall
  Houston, Texas

- HCA P & S West Paces Ferry Annex
- Rapha Treatment Center--Marietta
  Atlanta, Georgia

- HCA Pinebrook Hospital
  Reno, Nevada

- HCA South Arlington Medical Center
- Rapha Treatment Center--Bedford
  Arlington, Texas

- HCA Spring Branch Memorial Hospital
  Houston, Texas

- Sharpstown General Hospital
  Houston, Texas

- Youth For Christ Recovery Center
  Chicago, Illinois

Proposed New Sites

- ▲ Charlotte, North Carolina

- ▲ Denver, Colorado

- ▲ Ft. Lauderdale, Florida

- ▲ Kansas City, Kansas

- ▲ Los Angeles, California

- ▲ Lynchburg, Virginia

- ▲ New Orleans, Louisianna

- ▲ San Francisco, California

- ▲ Seattle, Washington

Finances, Insurance and Referrals

Referrals are accepted and encouraged from counselors, doctors, pastors and family members. Admissions Coordinators assess the criteria for admittance and make arrangements for hospitalization. RAPHA Adult and Adolescent Programs are covered by most major insurance companies. RAPHA does not bill patients for any services, since it functions to provide a management service to the hospital and act as a patient advocate. Final responsibility for all charges lie with the patient or guardian.

How to choose
a treatment program

RAPHA's treatment programs for psychiatric problems or substance abuse vary greatly from those of other facilities. It is very difficult to compare programs without first gaining specific information. General impressions of a treatment center through advertising, general reputation or casual word of mouth should not be the primary reason in choosing a treatment center.

If you need the services of an in-hospital psychiatric or substance abuse unit, here are some important questions you need to ask the admissions personnel of the hospital.

1. What are the qualifications of the staff performing therapies?

The qualifications should be master's level or above (M.S.W., M.A., M.S., Ph.D., Psy.D.), unless they are a C.A.D.A.C. (Certified Alcohol and Drug Abuse Counselor).

2. What is the unit nursing staff-to-patient ratio?

Unfortunately, hospitals often reduce staffing to save on costs. The ratios vary between a low of 1:6.25 patients to a high of 1:8 patients. (This means that for every 8 patients there is one staff member to care for them). The more staff, the more personalized the service.

3. What is the therapist-to-patient ratio?

These are the staff who do individual, group and family therapies. These ratios determine what the intensity of the program is and how much individual care you can expect. The ratios vary between 1:5 and 1:15 (Does not include therapists who do other types of therapy).

4. What are the total number of individual, group and family therapies scheduled each week?

If the therapist-to-patient ratio is very high, the therapy staff could not possibly have the time available for individualized treatment.

The patient may receive as little as an average of one to two hours of therapy per day.

5. How many times will the patient be seen by the psychiatrist? What are his charges?

The psychiatrist is an important part of any treatment. If he/she is not present, it is difficult to safely monitor the progress or present condition of the patient. Some facilities may only require the physician to make rounds twice per week.

6. Will the psychiatrist and hospital pre-agree to allow the patient to transfer to another psychiatrist or to another hospital if they or the family request the transfer?

Patients have found themselves being prohibited by their psychiatrist from transferring to the care of another doctor.

7. Is the hospital currently accredited by the Joint Commission on the Accreditation of Healthcare Organizations (JCAHO)?

Insurance companies do not typically pay hospitals who do not have this accreditation.

8. How do they keep illegal drugs off the unit?

Without stringent monitoring, drugs can be smuggled onto the unit. Many adolescent patients know which units in their city is the easiest for smuggling drugs and agree to go to these units. Find out if they perform any type of drug testing after outside visits.

9. Are radios and tape players with personal cassette tapes allowed on the unit?

Unfortunately some programs allow patients to bring rebellious or destructive music onto the unit, thus disrupting the environment. This is often the kind of music that has contributed to the problem.

10. Are TVs and VCRs monitored by the staff of the unit? Are "R"-rated movies shown on the unit?

Inappropriate shows have been common on some units, typically via the use of cable TV. If shows are not monitored, the patient may be exposed to extreme violence and explicit sex.

11. Is smoking allowed on the unit? If so, is it confined?

While it is difficult to prohibit smoking, many patients prefer to use non-smoking areas during leisure/therapy activities.

12. Is cursing or sexually suggestive language dealt with as inappropriate?

At times, instead of being a demonstration of behavior which is in need of correction, it is even tolerated. This is especially common on some chemical dependency units.

13. Is the expression of religious convictions such as Bible study and prayer encouraged by staff therapists or doctors?

14. Are pastors or clergy allowed to visit the patient? What is the protocol for arranging these visits?

15. What is done to help the patient afford the cost of treatment?

In addition to asking the questions listed above, we suggest that you make a copy of page 21 and have the admissions personnel fill it out and sign it as an assessment of the services they will provide.

Other hospital's response
to the previous 15 questions

1.Staff qualifications?_____

       Masters Level?   Yes   No

       CADACs?   Yes   No

2. Nursing staff-to-patient ratio:_____

3. Therapist-to-patient ratio:_____

4. Therapies:

       Individual range: ____to____times a week

       Group range: ____to____times a week

       Family range: ____to____time a week

5. Individual seen by psychiatrist   ____to____times a week;

       Charges range $ ____to____

6. Agree to transfer?   Yes   No

7. JCAHO accredited?   Yes   No

8. Drug Testing?_____

_____

9. Personal music?   Yes   No

10. TVs monitored?   Yes   No

11. Smoking?   Yes   No

       Confined?   Yes   No

        If yes, where?_____

12. Cursing discouraged?   Yes   No

13. Religious expression encouraged?   Yes   No

14. Clergy allowed to visit?   Yes   No

15. Help with affording costs?   Yes   No

Hospital Admissions Staff:

Signed_____

Date_____

RAPHA answers for hospital
treatment program

1. Staff qualifications? **Ph.D.'s, Ed.D.'s, and M.S.W.**

       Masters Level?   (Yes)   No

       CADACs?   (Yes)   No

2. Nursing staff-to-patient ratio: **1:4.7**

3. Therapist-to-patient ratio: **1:5 adult, 1:6 adolescent**

4. Therapies:

       Individual range: **3** to **5** times a week

       Group range: **14** to **21** times a week

       Family range: **1** to **2** times a week

5. Individual seen by psychiatrist   **3** to **6** times a week;

       Charges range $ **60** to **115**

6. Agree to transfer?   (Yes)   No

7. JCAHO accredited?   (Yes)   No

8. Drug Testing? **Rapid Eye Check, urine testing, searches - specific and random**

9. Personal music?   Yes   (No)

10. TVs monitored?   (Yes)   No

11. Smoking?   (Yes)   No

    Confined?   (Yes)   No

    If yes, where? **to adult units**

12. Cursing discouraged?   (Yes)   No

13. Religious expression encouraged? (Yes)   No

14. Clergy allowed to visit?   (Yes)   No

15. Help with affording costs? (Yes)   No

Hospital Admissions Staff:

Signed   *Robert S. McGee*

President, RAPHA

1-800-227-2657

Who needs RAPHA?

The criteria below are standards set by the Joint Commission on the Accreditation of Healthcare Organizations and the insurance industry.

Here is a guide that will help you make an educated decision when recommending treatment.

1. Is the person deemed to be dangerous to himself/herself or others?

Of course, if the individual is suicidal, homicidal, or involved in the destruction of property, that person most certainly needs the intensive care offered in a hospital setting.

2. Is the person involved in self-defeating behaviors?

Behaviors such as fire-setting, sexual promiscuity, running away, substance abuse (including alcohol), eating disorders (anorexia nervosa, bulimia), etc., should be viewed as grounds for hospital treatment.

3. Is reality testing impaired to the extent that activities of daily living are severely disordered?

Here we are talking about poor judgment, lack of love (emotionally flat), loss of memory, lack of orientation, severe depression, and extreme hyperactivity. These symptoms indicate the need for hospitalization.

4. Does treatment and/or pharmacological management require skilled observation?

If the person needs medication in order to deal with problems, or if the person needs medication adjustment, then hospitalization should be seriously considered.

5. Has outpatient therapy failed?

Persons who have been through outpatient therapy without success probably need the more thorough level of treatment offered in a hospital setting.

6. Is the person too acutely ill for outpatient treatment?

If the individual is psychotic, delusional, paranoid, phobic or suffering from hallucinations (either aural or visual), he/she should definitely be hospitalized for treatment.

7. Has the person demonstrated an inability to function in the home, in vocational pursuits such as school or extracurricular activities?

If so, the individual could certainly benefit from a hospital treatment program.

8. Has the person's symptoms worsened due to the collapse of his/her support systems?

If symptoms have worsened due to the deterioration of family, job, church, relationships, etc., the individual needs to be admitted to a hospital program.

Overcoming obstacles

Patient's Advocate. RAPHA admissions counselors represent the patient and family in all areas of admission to a unit. These counselors perform the majority of financial discussions, transportation arrangements and patient escort services. Simply stated, they handle the details.

Financial. RAPHA assists in determining the cost of treatment, then functions to reduce the out-of-pocket expenses to a level that is manageable by the family. Some payment by the family is normally required, but most often RAPHA either pays the hospital a significant portion not covered by insurance, or negotiates a reduction of the total charges based on the financial ability of the patient. This allows for resolution of the financial burden incurred by receiving help.

Transportation and Escort. Some patients live hundreds of miles from the nearest RAPHA facility, but they recognize the need for Christ-centered care, and will need to travel. RAPHA typically covers the entire cost of airfare and ground transportation to and from the hospital. Because it is important for family involvement in treatment, we assist financially in the travel expenses and hotel arrangements of the patient escort as well. This resolves all transportation issues.

As you can see, RAPHA is attempting to deal positively with obstacles in order to provide necessary Christ-centered care at one of our hospital or treatment centers. If you need help or if you want to help someone, call RAPHA today. Our Admission Counselors are standing by 24 hours a day to receive your call. 1-800-227-2657

William E. Stone, M.D.

Dr. Stone is the National Medical Consultant for Rapha. He received his medical degree from LSU and is a former faculty member of Harvard and Boston University. Dr. Stone is currently a faculty member at Georgetown University, Director of the Children and Adolescent Unit at Harris County Psychiatric Center and a visiting professor at the University of Texas Medical School in Houston.

1. What has been your observation of RAPHA's concern for patient care?

I have been very impressed with the commitment to providing the best of care to patients. The RAPHA staff actively supports a comprehensive quality assurance program that is designed to provide continuous monitoring and review of patient care and treatment outcome.

2. What do you say to those who believe that an emphasis on spiritual values during psychiatric treatment is inappropriate?

Psychiatric treatment should, whenever possible, be designed to assist the patient to cope within his or her individual environment. In this context, social, spiritual and cultural issues are of major significance in achieving an optimal result from treatment. The RAPHA program endeavors to utilize the patient's existing value and belief system to facilitate the treatment.

3. Is it possible to have a Christ-centered approach and be professional at the same time?

Yes. Professional treatment should be conducted so as to make use of any strengths the patient may have. Religious conviction is a strength and should neither be ignored nor considered a deterrent to effective treatment. A healthy value system that can be encouraged by the therapist is a great asset toward recovery.

Current Research Validates
The RAPHA Approach

1. *Religious involvement is negatively correlated with social
    problems, such as sexual permissiveness, drug abuse, and
    alcohol use, and is slightly negatively correlated with deviant or
    delinquent acts* (Burkett and White, 1974) Burkett, S.R. and
    White, M. Hellfire and Delinquency: Another Look. Journal for
    the Scientific Study of Religion, 1974, 13, 455-462.

2. *93% of Americans state a religious preference, 55% rank
    religion as very important in their lives, 69% belong to a church
    or synagogue* (Religion in America. Princeton, N.J.: The Gallup
    Organization and Princeton Religion Research Center, 1981).

3. *None of mental health groups (psychologists, psychiatrists, and
    social workers) can be considered very religious when compared
    to national norms (43% APA)* American Psychiatric Association
    Task Force Report 10: Psychiatrist's Viewpoints on Religion
    and their Services to Religious Institutions and the Ministry,
    1975, Washington D.C., A.P.A.

4. *(5% of American Psychological Association believed in God)*
    Ragan, C.P., Malong, H.N. and Beit-Hallahmi, B.
    Psychologists and religion: professional factors related to
    personal religiosity. Paper presented at the meeting of the
    American Psych. Assoc., Washington, D.C., September, 1976.

5. *Listed below are six fears of conservative Christian clients
    relative to secular counseling. Conservative Christians prefer
    like-minded counselors and distrust secular counselors*
    (Worthington, E.L., Jr. and Scott, G.G. Goal selection for
    counseling with potentially religious clients by professional and
    student counselors in explicitly Christian or secular settings.
    Journal of Psychology and Theology, 1983, 11, 318-329.

    A. *Ignore spiritual concerns*
    B. *Treat spiritual beliefs and experiences as pathological or
       merely psychological*
    C. *Fail to comprehend spiritual language and concepts*
    D. *Assume that religious clients share nonreligious cultural
       norms (e.g., premarital cohabitation, intercourse, etc.)*
    E. *Recommend "therapeutic" behaviors that clients consider
       immoral (e.g., experimentation with homosexuality)*
    F. *Make assumptions, interpretations, and recommendations
       that discredit revelation as a valid epistemology*

6. *Fear having values changed and misunderstood or being misdiagnosed because of beliefs* (Beutler, 1979) Beutler, L.E. Values, beliefs, religion and the persuasive influence of psychotherapy. Psychotherapy: Theory, Research and Practice, 16, 432-440.

7. *Religious value similarity between counselors and clients certainly affects therapy, but the relationship is not simple* (Worthington, E.) Religious counseling: a review of published empirical research. Journal of Counseling and Development, 1986, 64, 421-431.

8. *Religious clients who undergo counseling with counselors who have familiar values...experience a strengthened faith. The more Christians agreed with the doctrines of the Church, the less likely they were to seek professional counseling.* King, R.R., Jr. Evangelical Christians and professional counseling: A Conflict of Values? Journal of Psychology and Theology, 1978, 6, 226-281.

9. *The fact that therapists are less religious than are their clients suggests an erosion of religious beliefs.* Bergin, A.E. Psychotherapy and religious values. Journal of Consulting and Clinical Psychology, 1980, 48, 642-645.

10. *People preferred treatment plans that reflected an approach to religion that was similar to their own.* Dougherty, S.G. and Worthington, E.L., Jr. Preferences of conservative and moderate Christians for four Christian counselors' treatment plans for a troubled client. Journal of Psychology and Theology, 1982, 10, 346-354.

11. *Religious values may be more important in religious client's selection of a counselor than in their continuing with a counselor once counseling begins.* Haugen, C.D. and Edwards, K.J. Religious values and their effect on the perception of a therapist in a psychotherapy analogue. Journal of Psychology and Theology, 1976, 4, 160-167.

12. *Clients prefer counselors who have values similar to their own.* Worthington, E. Religious counseling: a review of published empirical research. Journal of Counseling and Development, 64, 421-431.

To Order Additional Products

In addition to the *Search For Significance* book and book/workbook, **Rapha Publishing** also offers a *Search For Significance Leader's Guide.* The guide is a series of 13 comprehensive small group sessions for a group study and discussion format and is written specifically for a person who has never led a small group.

Pricing

Book... $ 6.00 ea.

Book/Workbook................................ $ 12.00 ea.

Leader's Guide................................ $ 3.00 ea.

Include your name, address and zip code for shipment.

All prices include shipping.

Thank you for your interest in helping to share these important truths.

R A P H A   P U B L I S H I N G

P.O. BOX 580355
HOUSTON, TEXAS 77258